PROFILES IN CHRISTIAN COURAGE

PROFILES IN CHRISTIAN COURAGE

Extraordinary Inspiration for Everyday Life

Kerry Walters

ROWMAN & LITTLEFIELD
Lanham • Boulder • New York • London

Published by Rowman & Littlefield
A wholly owned subsidary of
The Rowman & Littlefield Publishing Group, Inc.
4501 Forbes Boulevard, Suite 200, Lanham, Maryland 20706
www.rowman.com

16 Carlisle Street, London W1D 3BT, United Kingdom

British Library Cataloguing in Publication Information Available

Library of Congress Cataloging-in-Publication Data
Walters, Kerry S.
Profiles in Christian courage : extraordinary inspiration for everyday life / Kerry Walters.
pages cm
Includes bibliographical references and index.
ISBN 978-1-4422-2331-8 (cloth : alk. paper) — ISBN 978-1-4422-2332-5 (electronic) 1. Christian biography. 2. Courage. I. Title
BR1700.3.W35 2014
270.8'20922—dc23
[B]
2014008856

∞ ™ The paper used in this publication meets the minimum requirements of American National Standard for Information Sciences Permanence of Paper for Printed Library Materials, ANSI/NISO Z39.48-1992.

Printed in the United States of America

To Kim Daubman
A woman of great courage

CONTENTS

Preface   ix

1 Who Would True Valor See   1

PART I: PHYSICAL COURAGE   13
2 Michael Lapsley   15
3 The Fraternal Martyrs of Burundi   23
4 Dorothy Stang   31
5 Alexander Men   39
6 The Tibhirine Monks   47
7 Mychal Judge   55

PART II: MORAL COURAGE   63
8 Ruth Manorama   65
9 Shahbaz Bhatti   73
10 The Nickel Mines Amish   81
11 Li Ying   89
12 Emil Kapaun   97
13 Clarence Jordan   105

PART III: SPIRITUAL COURAGE   115
14 Dianna Ortiz   117
15 Walter Ciszek   127

16 Thea Bowman   135

17 C. S. Lewis   143

18 Henri Nouwen   151

19 Mother Teresa   159

20 Everyday Courage for Everyday Christians   167

Notes   177

Index   189

PREFACE

This is a book about Christian courage and about courageous Christians. Life can be hard at times, and so can being a follower of Christ. That's why courage, or what I call here (riffing off of an expression coined by Ernest Hemingway) "Grace under pressure," is so important. To face the physical, moral, and spiritual dangers that confront us, whether they explode in extreme situations or emerge as everyday challenges, we Christians require the kind of fortitude that ultimately comes from aligning our will with God's. For most of us, this is easier said than accomplished. In this book, I offer some guidance on how to go about it, and I profile eighteen Christians (or groups), some famous and some lesser well known, who have done so. They are inspiring role models for the rest of us to keep in mind when the going gets rough in our own lives.

While this book was still in an early stage, I was privileged to meet Erin Youngbar, a young woman from Maryland who will forever be for me an exemplar of Christian courage. She's in her thirties, is a loving wife and mother of three young children, and has a faith whose strength astounds and humbles me. She's also a cancer patient who has undergone months of sometimes brutal radiation and chemotherapy for a brain tumor. Throughout the entire ordeal, beginning with the news of her diagnosis, she has kept a blog in which she candidly records her sorrow and occasional moments of despair, her fear, and her bewilderment at what's befallen her. But what comes through again and again, from the first to the latest entry, is an overwhelming courage bolstered by her trust in God, her struggle to live and love deeply as God lives and loves, and her determination to remain loyal to Christ, come what may. Her online journal can be found at http://erinyoungbar.com. It is a remarkable testimony to the power of Grace under pressure, and it has taught me a good deal of what it means to be a courageous Christian. Thank you, Erin.

1

WHO WOULD TRUE VALOR SEE

seeking Grace under pressure

John Bunyan, the seventeenth-century Puritan who wrote *Pilgrim's Progress*, knew something about Christian courage, or what he called "valor." Arrested numerous times and imprisoned on two separate occasions for nonconformity to the Church of England, he remained unbrokenly steadfast to his convictions. Not long before his death, he penned the only hymn he ever wrote as a tribute to the importance of courageously staying the course as a Christian wayfarer. It summed up his whole adult life.

> Who would true Valor see
> Let him come hither;
> One here will Constant be,
> Come Wind, come Weather.
> There's no Discouragement,
> Shall make him once Relent,
> His first avow'd Intent,
> To be a Pilgrim.

To the contemporary American ear, Bunyan's tribute to Christian courage might come across as a bit of quaint piety from a bygone age. Christianity in the United States seems pretty secure today, troubled by neither dangerous winds nor ominous weather. There's no social onus, much less danger, in being an American Christian. The days in which it was perilous to profess faith in Christ are gone, at least in the Northern

Hemisphere. Valorous constancy may've been called for in Bunyan's day, but it just doesn't seem to be applicable to us today.

But what if we're wrong? What if being a Christian always and everywhere requires valor, and that things have gone terribly wrong somewhere along the line if we've lost sight of that truth? What, in other words, if a Christianity that no longer requires courage has ceased to be the genuine article?

The nineteenth-century Danish writer Soren Kierkegaard thought so. Although an intensely religious man, he leveled a rebuke at the "respectable" Christianity of his own time that still stings today. Modern Christianity in the West, said Kierkegaard, costs nothing. The easiest thing in the world is to be a Christian. All one has to do is claim the label for oneself and presto!—one's automatically in the club. It's not necessary to attend church, pray, read the Bible, or even take Jesus's life and teachings to heart. As Kierkegaard noted, "Many people think that the Christian commandments (for example, to love one's neighbor as oneself) are purposely a little too rigorous—something like the household alarm clock that runs a half-hour fast so one does not get up too late in the morning."[1] If Christianity is so hassle-free and user-friendly that Jesus's words can be interpreted to suit our convenience, what possible need could there be for courage?

But Kierkegaard insisted that the feel-good and all-too-common variety of Christianity in his day (and ours) isn't the real deal. "If your ultimate and highest purpose is to have life made easy and sociable, then never have anything to do with Christianity," he warned, because genuine Christianity is a hard business that calls for a great deal of courage.[2] Without it, how many of us would be able to love those who despise us, affirm joy in times of sorrow, practice patience under trial, remain firm in the chaos of despair, or steady in the face of skepticism and hostility? Without courage, how many of us could, like Bunyan's Pilgrim, stay the course? We often say that love, joy, patience, and steadfastness are the gifts of faith. But without courage, no person would dare commit to the Faith in the first place. Without courage, no one could live the Faith. And without courage, no one would be willing to suffer persecution, much less to die, for the Faith. Fidelity to the real Christ, not the comfortable idol we too frequently substitute for him and whom Kierkegaard scorned, demands valor. It's no surprise that scripture encourages us again and again, "Be not afraid!"

COURAGE AS GUTS

But what does it mean for a Christian to practice courage? Surely the valor it takes to follow Jesus is no different than garden variety, generic valor. Courage is courage, right? Wrong.

From as far back as recorded history stretches, courage has typically been associated with a set of qualities that can best be labeled "manliness." (The Latin, Old French, and Middle English roots of "valor" actually denote masculine strength. By comparison, a coward in today's English is often called a "sissy," derived from the obviously feminine "sister.") Courage was understood as iron-willed resistance to a physical threat, a refusal to be cowed by danger or to flee from it. The physically powerful and merciless warrior who laughs at pain and hardship became the exemplar of courage. The Sumerian hero Gilgamesh and Homer's Achilles are valorous because they go out of their way to confront and subdue monsters and enemies, even at the risk of their own lives. Sometimes their courage is in the service of others, but just as often they perform deeds of valor to gain glory for themselves. Their courage is a two-fisted, riotously defiant kind that one associates with a larger-than-life masculinity.

This understanding of courage is still popular today. When we think of courage, the image of soldiers in battle, descendants of Gilgamesh and Achilles, is typically the first thing that pops into our heads. It's why action movie and video game heroes are so attractive to so many viewers and players. The loner cowboy who faces the gang of bad guys in a gunfight—think John Wayne here—or the hard-edged vigilantes in the *Rambo* and *Die Hard* film franchises who go up against impossible odds: these are modern-day exemplars of courage as manliness.

Over the centuries, this warrior model of courage has been complemented, but certainly not replaced, by a more subtle version of manliness. We've come to recognize that although courage sometimes is a resistance to physical threats, at other times it means a willingness to defy convention or popular opinion for the sake of what's right. The battlefield warrior displays one kind of valor and the conscientious dissenter another, but both of them still exhibit the same qualities traditionally associated with manly courage. Robert Jordan, the Spanish Civil War soldier in Hemingway's *For Whom the Bell Tolls* comes to mind as an example of the first, and Atticus Finch in Harper Lee's *To Kill a*

Mockingbird illustrates the second. Jordan's courage is in the manly use of his fists and the weapons of war; Finch's courage is in his manly defiance of bigotry. Although as a culture we're finally acknowledging that women also display remarkable courage, the kinds of qualities we praise in valorous women, especially female combat soldiers, are echoes of the ancient standard of manliness.

Ernest Hemingway coined an expression that seems to capture what lies at the heart of this conventional understanding of manly courage. Courage, or "guts," as he called it, is "grace under pressure."[3] When confronted with danger or a threatening challenge, whether it's physical or otherwise, the person with guts doesn't panic or fall into hysteria or back down. Calmly, with cool deliberation and unshakeable resolve, he deals with the situation, and does so without showy self-promotion. Someone who displays grace under pressure demonstrates that he possesses strong character and is independent, self-reliant, assertive, and confident. He's in charge of his own destiny. He lets the world know that he can handle himself in tight spots. He isn't someone to be messed with.

I don't for a moment want to suggest that this "guts" understanding of courage is false or ignoble, although I do think that it risks encouraging macho attitudes and acts that are more bullying and arrogant than genuinely courageous. Obviously, it can inspire people to perform valorous and even heroic deeds in dangerous situations. But it falls short of adequately capturing the kind of courage that Christians are called to practice. Christian courage isn't Hemingway's "grace under pressure." Instead, it's "*Grace* under pressure," a significant difference indeed.

COURAGE AS DIVINE GRACE

What sense can we make of the Grace under pressure that Christian courage is? A first-century Syrian bishop offers us a clue.

Ignatius, bishop of Antioch, was swept up in the wave of Christian persecution launched by the Roman emperor Trajan. While on his way to Rome and a savage death in the Colosseum—he was torn to pieces by wild beasts—the aged Ignatius wrote seven letters that are some of the earliest extant documents of the Church. In one of them, he spoke frankly about the doom toward which he was headed.

In ironic anticipation of the way he would die, Ignatius wrote that throughout the long journey to Rome he was chained to "ten leopards," a reference to the detachment of soldiers guarding him, who like wild beasts "proved themselves the more malevolent for kindness showed them." They seemed to delight in mocking and beating him. But, Ignatius assured his readers, he was not downcast. Let all the instruments of agony and death torment him—"Fire, cross, struggles with wild beasts, wrenching of bones, mangling of limbs, crunching the whole body, cruel tortures inflicted by the devil"—provided only, he said, that he could put on Christ. "Him I seek who died for us. Once arrived there, I shall be a man. Permit me to be an imitator of my suffering God."[4]

"Once arrived there, I shall be a man": this is a quite different understanding of manly courage than we find in either Hemingway or popular culture. For the man with guts, courage is the drive to overcome and conquer threats or obstacles. It's the sheer willpower to push the self to face and subdue what it fears. Courage, in this sense, is a supreme act of self-assertion, self-creation, and self-aggrandizement. Its center of gravity is the personal will.

But for Ignatius, courage is anything but self-assertion. Its center of gravity lies not in the self but in God. It's precisely a surrender of the self to "Him [whom] I seek." Only when Ignatius imitates his suffering God—that is, subordinates his own will to God's ("Not my will," Jesus cries during his Passion, "but Yours!")—is he able to withstand the horrors Trajan has in store for him. Only then is he a person of courage, empowered by God to face whatever the empire can throw at him. Only then is he a "man"—or, more accurately, a human being. Christian courage is about renouncing, not asserting, personal will. When we display "guts," we inflate ourselves. But when we display Christian courage, we empty ourselves.

What does this mean? And why call it "Grace under pressure"?

The goal of the Christian disciple's life is so to conform him- or herself to the life and spirit of Christ that, as St. Paul says, it is "no longer I who live, but Christ, who lives within me" (Gal 2:20). The way for this identification with Christ has already been prepared by God, first because humans are made in the divine likeness and image (Gen 1:27), and second by the advent of Christ, the New Adam, the prototype of what humans can and should be, who offers a way out of our brokenness and revitalizes our potential. To use traditional language, our creation in God's likeness as well as the restoration of our original nature by the Christ-event, a restoration that once more puts us in right relation or "justifies" us to God, is "grace." It is a gift lovingly bestowed upon us by God. We can do nothing to earn it, because a gift, by definition, is a gratuitous token of love, not a reward or award for good deeds.

Although we can do nothing to coax God into giving us grace, it *is* up to us to choose how to receive it once it's offered. We're called to cooperate with grace by striving to grow into our potential Godlikeness. Sitting on one's hands and expecting God to do all the work isn't an option. As Jesus said, "Not everyone who says to Me, 'Lord, Lord,' will enter the kingdom of heaven, but he who does the will of My Father who is in heaven will enter" (Matt 7:21). Of course, we always have the freedom to reject the gift outright. But accepting it means working to conform to the presence of Christ within and to behave in the world in a way that allows the presence to shine through. This means emptying one's ego so that the indwelling Christ can shine forth, practicing the virtues embodied in Christ—as St. Gregory of Nyssa observed, "the goal of the life of virtue is to be like God"[5] —and willingly and even eagerly accepting a share in Christ's redemptive suffering if it becomes necessary to do so.

All three of these acts require courage. Self-denial comes easily to no one. We crave to be in charge of our lives, even though we usually make a hash of things when we try. Practicing Christ's virtues in the world not only means resisting the temptations that entice us away from our God-likeness, but also, in many instances, taking countercultural stands that cause us to suffer from scorn, discrimination, and in some cases even imprisonment or death. When we side with the poor and vulnerable against the powerful and arrogant, the peacemakers instead of the war-mongers, and those who embrace voluntary simplicity rather than opulence, we risk the same kind of fury that assailed Christ. But the pressure of these challenges, threats, and dangers, whether they arise from external foes or interior temptations, can be endured because we are strengthened by Christ's indwelling presence. This is the "Grace under pressure" that emboldened Ignatius of Antioch, and it continues to bolster Christians today when faced with frightening challenges.

THREE KINDS OF COURAGE

The guts and Grace models of courage are, then, fundamentally different from one another. But they do agree on a couple of points. The first is that being courageous isn't about being fearless. At times the warrior stereotype suggests otherwise, particularly in guns 'n' glory Hollywood movies, but this isn't courage as much as foolhardiness. Not recognizing and responding properly to a threat is either madness or thoughtlessness. The ancients knew that. Gilgamesh the courageous warrior fears death, as does brave Achilles. Both of them freely admit it, and for all their lust for glory and love of battle, refrain (usually) from rashness. Similarly, conscientious dissenters who valorously dare to speak truth to power fear being thrown into jail, or worse, for their pains. Their courage consists precisely in doing what's right even though they tremble at the realization of what might befall them. And although angels in the Bible tell mortals "Be not afraid!," what they're really saying is "Come what may, trust God!" They know full well that to be a human is to be susceptible to fear. As Jesus said, "In the world you have tribulation." But he also said, "Be of good cheer. I have overcome the world" (Mk 5:36). Courage's job isn't to liberate us from fear, but to help us cope with it.

The second point on which the guts and Grace camps concur is that different kinds of threats elicit corresponding acts of courage. One size doesn't fit all. As we've seen, when most people hear the word "courage," what immediately comes to mind is derring-do in the face of a physical threat such as war, criminal assault, or natural disaster. *Physical* courage, or what's often called "bravery," is the valorous response particularly suited to those kinds of dangers. We've also seen that there's another kind of courage called forth by a different threat. It's the valor of standing up for what's right in defiance of unjust convention or authority. This *moral* courage, sometimes called "steadfastness," is often more difficult than physical courage. The second puts life and limb on the line, but the first risks the loss of reputation, social standing, livelihood, friends, liberty, and even family. For many of us, losing them is worse than losing life itself.

Although both guts and Grace defenders recognize physical and moral courage, it should be clear by now that they disagree on what motivates either. The guts model appeals to a manly exercise of self-discipline and willpower, while the Grace model rests on the self-sacrificing relinquishment of personal will to Christ's. It's precisely this crucial difference that prompts advocates of the guts model to reject a third type of courage with which Christians are especially familiar. It's the valor that's called for when we experience a crisis that causes us to lose sight of and perhaps even faith in God. Regardless of what triggers these dark nights of the soul, as they're often called—a personal tragedy, feeling overwhelmed by evil in the world, a tumble into deadly sin— they're characterized by an acutely despairing sense of God's absence. In many ways the *spiritual* courage needed to face them is the hardest of all to muster, because the forlorn emptiness they bring is the most terrible of all dangers. Losing life is hard, losing reputation and family worse. But losing God? Unthinkable.

The Christian who displays spiritual courage simply (although there's nothing simple about it!) cleaves to the God she no longer believes in or feels utterly alienated from, hanging on or enduring until the despair lifts, even though, paradoxically, she has no *hope* that it will. This type of courage especially highlights the claim that Grace under pressure is the secret to Christian valor, for the person in despair at God's absence has absolutely no interior resources to combat the abyss into which she's fallen. It's only the grace of God that pulls her out of it. All she can do is crouch in the darkness and await God's return. Her position is reminiscent of another line from Hemingway, in which one of his characters, an old and rather worn-out man, wearily faces what he sees as the emptiness of the universe but nonetheless prays: "Hail nada, full of nada, nada is with thee."[6] A prayer of despair, perhaps, but a prayer nonetheless.

Jesus, who always and everywhere is the model for Christian comportment, himself exemplified all three kinds of valor: physical courage in enduring bodily torture and cruel death following his arrest by the Jewish authorities, moral courage when he defied Temple culture by chasing away the money lenders, and spiritual courage when, despite the shockwave of despair that overwhelmed him on the Cross, he nonetheless persevered to the end in his salvific mission. In each of these instances (and more: the wilderness temptations, his befriending of prostitutes and publicans, and so on), Jesus acted through and in accordance with the Father's will. Grace under pressure.

PROFILES IN CHRISTIAN COURAGE

Jesus is the supreme example of courage for Christians. But this doesn't mean that we can't be instructed and inspired by the Grace-fueled courage our fellow believers show in dealing with physical, moral, and spiritual dangers. We have a lot to teach and learn from one another.

In the chapters that follow, I offer profiles of eighteen courageous Christians. I'm more aware than I can say that eighteen is a paltry number when one stops to think of the millions of valorous Christians who have lived over the past two millennia. I hope that in some small way this book pays tribute to the spirit—or, better, the Spirit—that animated them.

Because of the mind-boggling number of people who could've easily been profiled in this book, the narrowing-down process was particularly tough. My only firm resolve was that everyone selected would be our contemporaries or near-contemporaries. Stories of courageous first-century martyrs, sixteenth-century Reformers, or even nineteenth-century saints can certainly be both instructive and inspiring. But those of us who are alive now are confronted with many challenges and dangers unique to our day and age, and it seemed to me important to hear from others who likewise faced them. Aside from this requirement, however, the Christians profiled here come from all walks of life, are a mixture of men and women from different parts of the world, and belong to Protestant, Catholic, and Orthodox traditions within the larger Christian family. Some of them are still living; others have passed on. A few are world famous, while others are less well known.

The profiles are divided into three sections. The first highlights Christians who are exemplars of physical courage. North American and European Christians who almost never face physical persecution for their faith oughtn't to assume, as we too often do, that Christians the world over are similarly safe from martyrdom. The twentieth century produced more Christian martyrs than the nineteen centuries that preceded it, and the twenty-first century has already gotten off to a grim start. The physically courageous Christians profiled here include an antiapartheid activist nearly killed by a letter bomb, several dozen young African students who chose death rather than disloyalty to Christ, an American nun murdered in Brazil in retaliation for her championship of economic and environmental justice, a Russian priest who defied Soviet repression to bring the word of God to his people, seven Trappist monks who risked death to offer hospitality to Algerian Muslims, and a Franciscan who died in the horror of 9/11.

The second section focuses on Christians who are exemplars of the moral courage that empowers people to stand up for what's right, even when it means challenging political and religious authority or majority opinion. It profiles an Indian woman who champions "untouchables," a Pakistani Christian who pled for religious tolerance from non-Muslims, a community of Pennsylvania Amish who dared to forgive a heinous crime instead of insisting on payback, a Chinese woman who has gone to prison for practicing a faith despised by her government and millions of her fellow countrymen, a POW chaplain whose steadfastness gave much-needed hope to his fellow prisoners, and a Baptist preacher who founded a racially integrated community in the South when it was both unacceptable and shockingly perilous to do so.

The book's final section offers portraits of Christians who have displayed remarkable spiritual courage in dealing with situations that either threatened to throw them into the abyss of despair or, in a few cases, actually did so. They include an Ursuline nun whose kidnapping, rape, and torture shattered her childlike innocence; a priest whose years of solitary confinement in a Soviet prison brought him to a crisis of faith; a woman who refused to succumb to despair despite a long and ultimately futile struggle with cancer; a famous author whose intense grief caused him to lose faith in the goodness of God; another whose deep loneliness and insecurity nearly destroyed him during a terrible breakdown; and a nun, known and venerated throughout the world, who suffered silently through a fifty-year dark night of the soul.

The perceptive reader will quickly notice that hard and fast distinctions can't be drawn between physical, moral, and spiritual courage. A Christian who displays one almost certainly displays the others as well. Standing up for what's right at the risk of public scorn often calls for physical and spiritual courage; the courage to risk one's life is frequently bolstered by moral and spiritual courage; and so on. All one need do to appreciate the interdependence of the three kinds of courage is to recall the remarkable experience of Ignatius of Antioch on his ill-fated journey to Rome. He displayed moral courage in remaining loyal to his God in the face of mockery; physical courage in willingly dying for

Christ; and spiritual courage in resisting the very natural temptation under such circumstances to despair.

But that being said, it's also important to keep in mind that all of us are endowed with our own set of particular talents and weaknesses which makes us temperamentally suited to resist some threats better than others. Some of us may have a greater stock of physical than spiritual courage, or of moral than physical. So even though none of the Christians in this book fit exclusively into a single category of courage, their particular gifts and personalities dispose them toward one more than the other two.

As Kierkegaard tells us, being faithful to our Christian calling isn't easy, and the frightening world in which we live makes the task even more difficult. But we can rest assured that Grace has prepared us to face any and all of the challenges that may come our way, both the big ones that the Christians profiled here confronted, and the everyday ones which the rest of us regularly face, and which we'll examine in chapter 20. We already have what we need, Grace under pressure, if we but realize it. "For God did not give us a spirit of fear, but of power, and of love, and of a sound mind" (2 Tim 1:7).

Part I

Physical Courage

2

MICHAEL LAPSLEY

binding up the wounds of the brokenhearted

It was late April 1990. Michael Lapsley, Anglican priest, professed brother in the Society of the Sacred Mission religious order, and member of the antiapartheid African National Congress (ANC), had just returned from his farewell party, thrown by his friends. He was about to leave a post in the Zimbabwean capital of Harare for a parish in Bulawayo, the country's second largest city. Looking through the day's stack of mail, he happened upon a manila envelope postmarked from South Africa. It contained a couple of religious magazines, one in English and the other in Afrikaans. When Lapsley opened the English one, he triggered the bomb hidden inside.

The blast should have taken off Lapsley's head, as it was clearly intended to do. It was powerful enough to knock down the ceilings in three rooms of his house and leave a large crater in the floor. But for whatever reason, the bomb maimed rather than killed him, blowing off both his hands, lacerating his face and chest with shrapnel, shattering his eardrums, and damaging his right eye so badly that it had to be removed later on. Rushed to hospital, Lapsley remained fully conscious as medics struggled to stop the bleeding. He was given no pain medication lest it interfere with the emergency surgery he would need. But because a skilled surgeon couldn't be immediately found, he suffered for several hours before finally going into the operating room.

Lapsley spent an entire month in the Harare hospital, and another seven in two Australian ones, enduring multiple surgeries aimed at putting him back together. His hearing gradually returned, he was fitted with a glass eye, and he learned to manipulate two prosthetic hands—clips, really, that ingeniously opened and closed when he flexed his shoulder muscles. He had to relearn how to do the simplest of everyday tasks: putting on eyeglasses, fastening buttons, manipulating typewriter keys. But from the very first, he refused to think of himself as a victim. While still in the Harare hospital, he told a friend that the people who sent the mail bomb to him had "got it wrong." They may have deprived him of his hands, "but I never really used my hands against them. I'm no good at shooting . . . I've still got my voice and that was always my weapon."[1] He would put that weapon to good use in the years to come.

The people who "got it wrong," as things turned out, were members of the euphemistically named Civil Cooperation Bureau (CCB), a secret South African government-sponsored organization, put together in 1986, to target and assassinate troublesome critics of apartheid. The CCB engaged in hits both domestically and abroad, using a variety of methods, including poison, bombs, and arson, to eliminate enemies of the state. It disbanded shortly after Lapsley's maiming, but not before its agents had murdered or conspired to murder thirty people.

Michael Lapsley, one of the CCB's last victims, was born in New Zealand in 1949. One of seven children, he entered the Society of the Sacred Mission when he was just seventeen. Young as he was, he longed even then for the society to send him to South Africa. Three or four years earlier, he had read Trevor Huddleston's *Naught for Your Comfort,* a damning indictment of apartheid by an Anglican priest whose parish was in South Africa. Persuaded by Huddleston that the South African repression of blacks was contrary to everything Christianity represented, young Lapsley was afire to do something to end apartheid. But he would have to wait until 1973 to finally step foot on South African soil, when the society sent him to Durban University to continue his studies and to serve as Anglican chaplain to students.

Lapsley went to South Africa as a pacifist. But after witnessing firsthand the brutal system of apartheid, he came to the conclusion that the situation was more morally complex than he had imagined. In the first place, he realized that by simply being a white person in South Africa, he "enjoyed and benefited from the fruits of violence in a system where pigmentation decided just how valuable your life is and how long you are likely to live."[2] So like it or not, he was already implicated in violence. Moreover, Lapsley soon saw that what counted as physical violence was rigged to favor South Africa's white population. When blacks used violence, it was "terror"; when white police did, it was "law and order." Finally, it became clear to Lapsley that a profession of pacifism was more a white luxury than a live possibility for black South Africans. "I came to the conclusion," he wrote, "that in the South African situation, for me to ask black people not to use the gun to help defend and liberate themselves, is to ask people to have a complicity in their own deaths."[3] Lapsley concluded that in a brutally oppressive system like apartheid, to preach Christian pacifism was to sanction a status quo that daily injured blacks.

Moving away from fidelity to Christian pacifism wasn't easy for someone who had been convinced from an early age that violence was abhorrent to Jesus. The tipping point for Lapsley was the Soweto massacre in June 1976. High school students from Johannesburg's Soweto township organized a protest march against a two-year-old law that mandated Afrikaans as the language of instruction in black schools. Police initially set dogs on the crowd and then, panicking at its swelling numbers, fired into it. Twenty-three students were killed, many of them shot in the back as they ran for cover. (Twenty-three was the officially reported number of casualties; independent estimates are closer to two hundred.) The massacre sparked nationwide protests that led to hundreds of arrests. Many of those taken into custody were tortured; some died while "resisting arrest" or "attempting to escape." Meanwhile, the entire nation went into lockdown. It became obvious to Lapsley that in the police state apartheid South Africa had become, nonviolent resistance was worse than ineffective.

After Soweto, Lapsley joined thousands of students across the country in denouncing the slaughter. His outspokenness thrust him into the national limelight and resulted in his election as national university chaplain, a post whose holder was determined by students rather than church authorities. Lapsley was soon visiting university campuses throughout the country condemning the Soweto massacre and calling for resistance to apartheid. He warned his Christian student audiences that doing nothing about apartheid was a betrayal of their faith. Standing around wringing one's hands wasn't an option; choices had to be made and action taken. As he wrote a few years afterward,

South Africa explodes the myth of the possibility of neutrality for the Christian or indeed for anyone else. The very nature of apartheid means that there is no middle ground. The system decides whether you will enjoy the oppression of the oppressor, or the oppression of the oppressed.[4]

Lapsley's public denunciations of apartheid not only brought him national coverage. They also made him visible for the first time to state authorities, who acted quickly to shut him up. Had he been a South African citizen, they may well have arrested him, or worse. But because he was a New Zealand national, they settled for refusing to renew his visa when it expired three and a half months after Soweto, effectively kicking him out of the country.

Barred from South Africa, Lapsley requested a church post in Lesotho, the small landlocked nation situated entirely within the borders of South Africa. Lesotho was an obvious choice for him because the tiny country had become a sort of underground railroad destination for apartheid resisters fleeing arrest. Shortly after settling there, Lapsley decided to request ANC membership. Given the notoriety of *Umkhonto we Sizwe*, or "Spear of the Nation," the ANC's armed wing, Lapsley's decision struck many of his fellow Christians as ominously misguided. Others, including not a few ANC members, thought it odd that a white man would ask to join what was popularly perceived as an all-black organization.

Actually, the ANC had always been biracial and had embraced non-violence for the first half-century after its founding in 1912. That ended in 1960 with the Sharpeville massacre, in which sixty-nine unarmed civilians protesting government-mandated restrictions on the movements of blacks were shot down. For the ANC, the killings were the final straw. Shortly afterward, Spear of the Nation was organized, and the now banned ANC adopted a new policy of violence against the apartheid system.

Critics of the new ANC charged that the tactics it embraced, such as targeting white civilians by planting bombs in places like nightclubs and shopping malls, were terroristic. Defenders deplored the need for violence, but insisted that it was the only effective weapon against a regime notorious for its merciless suppression of dissent. One of them was Lapsley. Shortly after his application for membership in the ANC was accepted, he himself wondered if membership in an organization that met violence with violence was compatible with his holy orders and thought seriously about leaving the church. It was one thing to intellectually recognize that nonviolence wouldn't work in South Africa; it was another thing to actively promote it. But he finally decided to remain a churchman, partly because he was disgusted by the allegedly biblical defenses of apartheid offered by many Afrikaans clergy and wanted to offer an alternative from the pulpit, and partly because he believed that the violence practiced by the ANC was a morally acceptable application of just war doctrine.

Although by no means endorsed by all Christians, just war doctrine has a long pedigree. Formulated by Augustine in the fourth century and refined by many theologians since, the position states that under certain conditions, armed conflict, while always regrettable, is ethically permissible. Lapsley saw the ANC's armed opposition to apartheid as a liberation struggle that satisfied the conditions for just war. He continued to acknowledge that nonviolence is "the morally superior way." But as he saw it, the South African state, itself "fundamentally violent," would never even recognize blacks as human beings, much less allow them fundamental human rights.[5] Consequently, armed resistance was the only option. In more than one speech during the years of his campaign against apartheid, Lapsley invoked Dietrich Bonhoeffer, the Lutheran pacifist who likewise had felt obliged to forsake nonviolence in the face of Nazi totalitarianism.

Lapsley was in Lesotho for nearly seven years, serving as warden at the Anglican seminary there. During that time he continued to be a very public critic of South African apartheid, speaking in a number of countries around the world to draw international attention to its injustices. His opposition earned him the wrath of white defenders of apartheid. It was during this period that he began receiving death threats; as early as 1980, he told a friend that he doubted he would survive the decade. Just as predictably, his outspokenness kept him in constant trouble with more timid authorities in the Anglican Church and even his own religious order. He moved on to Zimbabwe in 1983, after both government and church leaders in Lesotho decided that he was too obvious a target for them to protect—not to mention the fact that his mere presence endangered the well-being of those around him. In Zimbabwe, his active and public support of the ANC once more raised ecclesial hackles, and by the time he received the package bomb in

1990 he was on the outs with his bishop there, who had revoked his ministerial license in the hope of getting rid of him.

Ironically, the same year that Lapsley was nearly killed also saw a lifting of the ban on the ANC and Nelson Mandela's release from prison after serving a twenty-seven-year stretch. By the time Lapsley had returned to South Africa in 1992, apartheid had been officially repealed and preparations for the nation's first universal elections were well under way. Held in 1994, Lapsley, by this time a South African citizen, voted in them. Mandela was elected president by an overwhelming majority. A new day had dawned for South Africa.

Lapsley's maiming and long period of recovery, coinciding as they did with the collapse of apartheid, left him at loose ends. Although gratified by the new wind blowing through his adopted nation, it was also the case that his identity for the past two decades had revolved around resistance to apartheid. Now he found himself adjusting not only to the loss of his hands and an eye, but also to the cause that had infused his life with meaning. To make matters worse, he discovered on returning to South Africa that the Anglican Church was wary about finding him a position. His superiors thought him too hot, even after the end of apartheid, to take a chance on.

In what proved to be a move that he later regretted, Lapsley agreed to serve as director of the Theological Exchange Programme, an organization that promoted dialogue between South African and global Southern Christians in order to explore the relationship between faith and political liberation movements. But the organization had been badly run before Lapsley's arrival, and he inherited several ongoing feuds that hamstrung his ability to lead effectively. Within a year he was ready to move on and accepted a position as chaplain for a trauma center that offered pastoral and psychological counsel to victims of apartheid. Lapsley admitted that he floundered at the beginning, having little if any idea exactly what a chaplain in a trauma center was called to do. But of one thing he was sure: his own near brush with violent death offered him a radically new opportunity for ministry. He had been, as he said, a freedom fighter. Now he wanted to devote himself to healing others who had been maimed physically, emotionally, and spiritually. Liberation had been won. But the wounds of a half century of savage oppression endured.

Even before the South African Truth and Reconciliation Commission (TRC) convened in 1996, Lapsley and his colleagues began offering what they called Healing of Memories workshops. He recognized, as both a priest and a victim of trauma himself, how important it was for other victims to be given the opportunity to talk openly about what had happened to them and to "be recognized and honored for their sacrifices and suffering."[6] By 1998, it was clear that the TRC, chaired by Archbishop Desmond Tutu, simply couldn't provide all the tens of thousands of victims the healing they needed to begin to recover their lives. So Lapsley and several of his colleagues founded the independent Institute for Healing of Memories. The nonprofit foundation soon reached out to offer help to victims of other oppressive regimes and now conducts workshops in Europe, North America, and Australasia.

Ever since his own maiming by the defenders of apartheid, Lapsley resisted the temptation to sink into victimhood. To do so, he feared, would be to succumb to "hatred, bitterness, self-pity and desire for revenge," and this "would consume me. It would eat me alive."[7] Only three months after the bombing, he sent a letter to his friends, laboriously tapped out on a typewriter with his new "fingers," declaring his resolve to rise above his personal tragedy. "In my own body," he wrote, "I have experienced suffering and crucifixion, but I am also beginning to experience a taste of the new life which one day will come to us all in Southern Africa."[8] Five years later, he said in a radio interview that "God and people of faith and hope enabled me to make my bombing redemptive—to bring life out of the death, the good out of the evil. I was enabled to grow in faith, in commitment to justice, in compassion."[9]

Lapsley's aim in the Institute for Healing of Memories is for its workshops to help other victims transform their suffering into new life, just as he did. But healing isn't important for personal restoration only. For Lapsley, still ardently committed to working for justice, it's also a necessary condition for social transformation. "Unless we bind up the wounds of the brokenhearted," he writes, "we cannot hope to create a just and durable society where everyone has a place in the sun, for the victims of the past too easily become the victimizers of the future."[10]

Lapsley's journey from freedom fighter to bombing victim to healer has been sustained all along by what he calls his "simple childhood faith in a loving god and in Jesus who suffered like me and was crucified."[11]

The Jesus who is spat upon, beaten, maimed, and crucified, the same Jesus who resurrects to eternal life still carrying the marks of his trauma on the Cross, has been a continuous inspiration for Lapsley. In his speeches, interviews, and writings he frequently mentions an Eastern Orthodox icon of Christ that he once saw and has never been able to get out of his mind. It depicts a disabled Jesus who has one leg noticeably shorter than the other, a Messiah "who is not beautiful and comely to look at but rather one who is disfigured."[12] The icon, Lapsley said, became an important image for him to hold on to, symbolizing as it does the compatibility between wounds and strength, imperfection and holiness, external disfigurement and inner beauty. It's an image, and a message, that he's devoted the last three decades of his life to sharing with a hurting world.

3

THE FRATERNAL MARTYRS OF BURUNDI

they were singing psalms of praise

Do not resist one who is evil." "Love your enemies and pray for those who persecute you." All of us recognize these lines from the Sermon on the Mount. But for many of us, knowing them is one thing and acting on them quite another. We excuse ourselves by insisting that Jesus didn't mean to be taken literally or that he intended his remarks to describe the future Kingdom of Heaven, not the fallen world of men and women. Nation states, even those which claim to be founded on Christian values, likewise ignore Christ's words whenever it's to their advantage to go to war or to persecute dissidents within their borders.

No doubt part of the explanation for why we so often ignore Jesus's teachings is because they interfere with our self-serving desires and plans. But frequently we shy clear of them out of timidity and lack of resolve. Whenever we're confronted with real or imagined threats, our encoded response is, of course, fight or flight. Jesus's recommendation to renounce both by staying firmly anchored in him is a daunting prospect because it goes against our most primitive urges. So time and again we either lash out in fearful anger, or we flee in panic. In neither case do we pray for our enemies, much less love them. In neither case do we practice Christian courage.

But forty young men—little more than boys, actually—steeled themselves one terrifying morning in the spring of 1997 to remain loyal to Jesus's teaching in the Sermon on the Mount. They faced their enemies, neither fleeing in terror nor lashing out in defensive anger, and prayed for them even as they were cut down with bullets and grenades. Their story is a remarkable example of the kind of physical courage faith can inspire and sustain.

The boys were all students at Le Petit Seminaire de St-Paul, a Catholic boarding school in Buta, a rural area in the East Africa nation of Burundi. St-Paul, founded in 1965, provided a quality education to its students, many of whom went on to join the priesthood. At the time of the 1997 massacre, the school had some 250 students between the ages of eleven and nineteen.

Burundi, often called the "African Switzerland" because of its gorgeous landscape, is in the Great Lakes region of Africa, bordered to the north by Rwanda, to the west by Lake Tanganyika, and to the east by Tanzania and the Congo. In stark contrast to its natural beauty, Burundi is an impoverished nation, one of the globe's poorest and most densely populated. Part of its poverty is a consequence of the toll AIDS has taken on its populace. Six to ten percent of adults are infected.

The world gasped in horror at the 1994 genocide that devastated Burundi's neighbor, Rwanda. But it's generally unknown that a similar carnage had erupted in Burundi the previous year, and for largely the same reason. Both nations had been claimed as colonies by Germany in the late nineteenth century and subsequently turned over to Belgium at the end of World War I as part of the reparations settlement. Both were primarily populated by two distinct ethnic groups, the Tutsis and the Hutus. Even though the Hutus far outnumbered the Tutsis, both German and Belgian colonial authorities favored the taller and lighter skinned Tutsis, who were primarily herders of cattle, to the shorter and darker Hutus, who were mainly subsistence farmers. There had long been rivalry between the two groups, but the colonial privileging of one over the other ratcheted up the animosity to a new level.

Burundi became an independent nation in 1962, but for the next thirty years was ablaze with civil war as Hutus and Tutsis savagely fought one another for political dominance and sometimes out of sheer hatred for one another. The fighting waxed and waned over those three decades. Cease-fires were periodically declared only to be inevitably broken by one side or the other. But when a Tutsi faction assassinated a Hutu president in late 1993, a new cycle of violence erupted that lasted for a full ten years. Armed bands of Hutus and Tutsis roamed the Burundian countryside killing suspected enemies, destroying villages, and forcibly impressing recruits, many of whom were little more than children. An estimated 800,000 Burundians, Tutsis as well as Hutus, were driven from their homes, and another 300,000 slaughtered before an armistice was finally signed in 2003. The forty schoolboys at St-Paul were among the thousands of innocents who fell victim to the fighting.

The campus of St-Paul consisted of several buildings, including a two-storied dormitory, classrooms, and the church. The students who roomed and boarded there were both Tutsi and Hutu. Unlike many of their elders, they lived together in harmony, calling themselves a Christian fraternity or brotherhood. Shortly before the massacre, they had all gone on an eight-day Easter retreat which, in defiance of the turmoil that had raged throughout Burundi all their lives, had especially emphasized unity. The boys came away from the retreat aglow with love of God and one another. As one of their teachers said, they returned to the seminary "full of rejoicing and joy, the word in their mouths was 'God is good and we have met Him.' They spoke of heaven as if they had just come from it, and of the priesthood as if they had just been ordained."[1]

Things hadn't always been this way with them. Before coming to St-Paul many of the boys, born and raised in a nation embroiled in civil war, had absorbed the ethnic hatred poisoning the land. When the latest round of fraternal killing began in 1993, they grew wary and distrustful of one another. Many of them wanted to leave the seminary and join the fighting. But Father Zacharie Bakuru, the seminary's headmaster, worked hard to keep them together, constantly exhorting them to love one another as Christ loved them all, urging them to counteract the fraternal killing that was devastating the land with fraternal love based on their faith. The Easter retreat was Father Zacharie's most recent effort to protect the boys from the evil of hatred. Thanks to him, St-Paul remained one of the few ethnically integrated schools in Burundi during the 1990s.

On the evening of April 29, 1997, the boys said their prayers and fell asleep in their bunks to the patter of rain. Early the next morning, at around 5:30, they were awakened by the harsh rat-tat-tat of automatic gunfire. Two thousand Hutu soldiers of the CNDD, the misnamed National Council for the Defense of Democracy, had surrounded the seminary compound. Placing several gunners on ridges around the school, they peppered the buildings and windows with bullets. Then they attacked in three separate waves. Most of the CNDD soldiers had guns and grenades; many carried less sophisticated but still deadly weapons such as machetes, knives, and clubs.

Given the ongoing state of unrest in the country, seminary officials had thought it prudent to hire a small contingent of armed guards to deter possible marauders. But the guards quickly fled after one of them was killed in the initial CNDD assault. The seminary's instructors, including Father Zacharie, did their best to calm down the terrified students by reassuring them that the soldiers intended them no harm. They just managed to get the younger boys to a secure building before the second attack struck. From that moment on, although teachers as well as pupils under fifteen years of age remained safe, the older students were on their own and vulnerable.

One of the few survivors, Carter Ndayisaba, was asleep when the attack started. He remembers being awakened by gunfire that shattered windows in his dormitory and sent bullets into walls and ceilings. Many of the boys, including Carter, dived under their beds. A few others jumped through windows and tried to flee into the countryside, but were quickly captured. In a matter of minutes, soldiers stormed into the dormitory and began spraying the ceiling with bullets to intimidate the boys. Carter's memory is that the shooting lasted for almost five minutes. "And then," he recalled, "one of the leaders ordered us to come out of our hiding places [from under the beds]. He was saying 'The Tutsis to one side and the Hutus to the other side.'"[2]

It was pretty clear what was about to happen. The soldiers intended to slaughter the Tutsi students and forcibly draft the Hutu ones. Since the two ethnic groups have distinctive physical characteristics, the CNDD leader would've had no difficulty in identifying who was Tutsi and who was Hutu. The order for the boys to segregate themselves was a ploy to force frightened Hutus to publicly betray their Tutsi fellow students by deserting them.

The tactic backfired. Hutu seminarians refused to separate themselves from their Tutsi classmates. Blazing with the spirit of Christian fraternity lit by their Easter retreat, the youths showed that they had taken to heart the principle that in the Body of Christ, "there is neither Jew nor Greek, there is neither slave nor free, there is neither male nor female" (Gal 3:28). They locked arms, faced the soldiers' guns, and awaited their fate. One of the survivors remembered a classmate urging his fellows to be brave. "Hey, let's die like men," he said. "Let's die with dignity."[3]

The soldiers, not expecting such a reaction, were thrown off guard and uncertain about how to respond. But their commander, who happened to be a woman, was enraged by their hesitation. According to Jolique Rusimbamigera, another survivor, she leveled her machine gun at the boys, snarled, "Shoot the idiots who won't separate!," and began firing into them.[4] The soldiers quickly followed suit, and for a few horrible seconds the dormitory room was filled with the crackle and smoke of gunfire. When it ended, the concrete floor was covered in blood, and dead or wounded boys were lying in heaps. The soldiers left, ending the second wave of attack.

After the departure of the CNDD killers, those boys who had been only slightly wounded or who had managed to escape the volleys began tending those of their classmates who were seriously hurt. This in itself was another extraordinary act of physical courage, since they could've tried to flee. But the strength of their shared fellowship in Christ kept them at the scene of the carnage. Some of the wounded boys were in shock, and cried out, "Oh God! Have you abandoned us? Do you accept this? Look, we are dying like birds!"[5] But others consoled them, one survivor recalled, "by singing psalms of praise," while others repeated Jesus's words from the Cross: "Forgive them Lord, for they know not what they do." Still other boys prayed the rosary. Many of them were later found with their fingers clutched around their beads.

The CNDD soldiers, hearing the prayers, psalms, and cries of distress from the dormitory and realizing that some of the boys were still alive, returned a third time to finish them off. One of them lobbed a grenade into the room. Others stepped over bodies to shoot the wounded at pointblank range. By the time this final wave of killing ended, forty students were dead and forty more wounded, many of them with horrible injuries. Only three of the boys trapped in the dormitory that morning escaped unscathed. Eight of the murdered students were from Rwanda, six from the Congo, one from Nigeria, and the rest from Burundi.

In the days that followed, television news reports about the attack shocked Burundians with chilling footage of rows of blanket-covered bodies. The people who lived in Buta, many of whom had sons at St-Paul, were initially stunned and then angry; ethnic violence between local Hutus and Tutsis threatened to explode. Father Zacharie put aside his own intense grief at the tragedy in his school to devote himself over the next few weeks to calming the situation. He urged the outraged friends and relatives of the boys to honor their sacrifice by emulating their refusal to return evil for evil. Thanks to his efforts at reconciliation, the province of Buta remained relatively untouched by reprisals after the massacre.

The slain boys were buried on the school grounds, in two parallel rows of white-tiled tombs marked with crosses painted red to commemorate their martyrdom. The damage inflicted on the school buildings by grenades and shells was gradually repaired, but some bullet holes were deliberately left as a memorial of what happened. Forty days after the massacre, the school church was rededicated to Mary, Queen of Peace. In the months that followed, one of its walls was decorated with a large mural depicting each of the forty young martyrs. According to one of the church's priests, the church has become "a place of pilgrimage where Burundians come to pray for reconciliation of their people, for peace, conversion, and hope for all." He believes that the slain boys' "testimony of faith, unity, and fraternity" commemorated in the Mary, Queen of Peace Church, sends "a message for humankind, and their blood become[s] a seed for peace in our country and the world."[6]

For his part, Father Zacharie found little peace in the immediate aftermath of the tragedy. Emotionally shattered by the killing as well as the grueling strain of ministering to the grief-stricken families of the boys, he left Burundi for France a few months after the attack. The traumatized priest sought refuge in a Benedictine monastery, probably intending to remain there, far from the violence of his native land, for the rest of his life. But three years later he felt a call to return to the very site of the massacre as the founding abbot of a Benedictine monastery built adjacent to the school. He remains there to this day, another example of Christian courage.

Some commentators on global affairs, especially those unsympathetic to the claim of many international rights organizations that Christians in developing nations increasingly endure persecution, have been quick to point out that the boys of St-Paul were killed because of ethnic hatred, not because of their faith.[7] But although this is technically correct, it misses the deeper significance of the tragedy. The nearly eighty schoolboys either killed or horribly wounded on that fateful day in April chose death because they refused to betray the Christian fellowship to which they had pledged themselves. The CNDD soldiers who shot them down may have been motivated by ethnic hatred, but the way in which the students accepted and met their fate was motivated by Christian commitment. It was born of the courage that comes from the realization that in the end, nothing can truly harm the person who clings to Christ. If we lovingly bear his Cross, we gloriously participate in his Resurrection.

That love not only enabled the fraternity martyrs to die singing psalms and tending to one another. It also allowed the survivors to pray for the souls of their attackers. Jolique Rusimbamigera spoke for all of them. "I pray," he said, "that the sacrifice of the murdered students and our suffering will lead the soldiers who caused this suffering to their own conversion."[8]

4

DOROTHY STANG

I know they want to kill me

By 2004, she had lived in Brazil for nearly four decades, helping small farmers in the Amazon to resist the encroachments of wealthy landowners and working to safeguard the rain forests against slash-and-burn agriculture. She had earned a reputation over the years as a fearless and determined advocate, and had recently been recognized with a couple of humanitarian awards. But it was her first time on Brazilian national television.

Seventy-three-year-old Dorothy Stang, a nun of the Sisters of Notre Dame de Namur, arrived at the TV studio to participate in a televised panel discussion about deforestation in the Amazon and the oppression of peasant farmers. She showed up wearing a shirt that had the slogan "Death of the forest is death of us all" stenciled on it. Compared to the talking heads and public policy wonks who were the other panelists, she seemed slightly threadbare.

Sister Dorothy sat quietly listening to her fellow panelists discuss the plight of the small farmers who were bullied and terrorized by powerful landowners eager to seize their holdings. Then the moderator turned to her as someone who worked firsthand with the peasants and asked if she knew specifically who the aggressors were. Stang's response electrified Brazil. "I have lived in [the Amazon] for twenty years," she said. "I know who has land documents that are forged and those that are real . . . and the forgers outweigh the legitimate ones." Then she reached into the cloth bag she always carried, pulled out a sheet of paper, and read off a long list of the offending ranchers as well as the crooked cops they had in their pockets. Some of the names on Stang's list were cronies of government officials and captains of Brazil's economy.[1]

Less than a year later, Sister Dorothy was dead, shot down on the orders of furious ranchers who feared her advocacy of both the farmers they sought to dispossess and the rain forest they hoped to exploit. Stang had known for some time that her life was in grave danger. Toward the end, she received multiple death threats. At least one Brazilian newspaper reported that she was in the "crosshairs" of the powerful ranchers. Friends, family, and coworkers advised her to leave Brazil. But she refused. "I know they want to kill me," she wrote a friend, "but I will not go away. My place is here alongside these people who are constantly humiliated by others who consider themselves powerful . . . I have learned that faith sustains you."[2]

Dorothy Stang's ministry and eventual martyrdom in Brazil was far removed in both place and time from the small Ohio town where she was born in 1931. Her family was large—nine children in all—and devoutly Catholic. Her father was an engineer by profession, but a farmer at heart. During the Great Depression, when money was scarce, he plowed up most of the household's yard to plant vegetables, and enlisted all the Stang kids each growing season in preparing the soil, planting, weeding, and harvesting. He refused to use chemical fertilizers on his plot, preferring instead natural manures. Dorothy learned at an early age the importance of caring for the earth in a sustainable way.

When she was sixteen years old and still in high school, Dorothy—or "Dot," as family and friends called her all her life—heard a nun of the Sisters of Notre Dame de Namur lecture on Catholic missions in China. She decided that she wanted to join the order, whose particular ministry was teaching impoverished children around the globe. She entered a rigorous seven-year course of training and became a full-fledged sister in 1951. Her order sent her to Chicago for a couple of years to work as an assistant teacher before assigning her to a school near Phoenix, Arizona. During the weekdays, Sister Dorothy taught relatively privileged white students. But on weekends, she tutored the children of Mexican migrant workers who harvested grapes and lettuce on the huge farms surrounding Phoenix. She picked up their language pretty quickly, and it wasn't unusual for her to join them in the fields, working alongside them whenever she had a free afternoon. One of her particular worries was their exposure to chemical pesticides from crop-dusting planes.

Sister Dorothy was named principal of her school in 1963. But she had never forgotten that her first attraction to religious life was the prospect of missionary work in the developing world. So when she heard two years into her new job that her order was looking for volunteers to teach in Brazil, she jumped at the chance. She arrived in South America in September 1966, and never looked back.

Sister Dorothy had encountered poverty among the migrant farm worker communities in Arizona, but she was unprepared for the abject living conditions the bulk of Brazilians endured. Most of the nation's labor force was agricultural. Workers on huge *fazendas* or ranches were paid such poor wages, and were generally in such debt to their employers, that they lived in a state of virtual slave peonage. It was the lucky peasant who managed to arrange a crop-sharing arrangement with the large farm owners. It was the rare peasant who owned a plot of land he could call his own.

On her arrival, Sister Dorothy's home base was a small city of twelve thousand in northeastern Brazil. She and a handful of other nuns were charged with taking some of the pressure off the local priests by helping to baptize and marry the locals and, most important, making home visits. Their responsibilities within the city alone were burdensome. But to add to them, the sisters also had to travel to the scattered villages and settlements in the forests that surrounded the city. They were often so far out in the boondocks that it took a day or more for Stang and her companions to reach them.

Recognizing that there were too many settlements too widely apart to visit on a regular basis, Stang began organizing local base communities in which villagers met to discuss how the Bible related to their hard lives, to pray together, and to offer one another mutual support. In order to win the peasants' trust, Sister Dorothy and her fellow nuns decided to live like them by renouncing many creature comforts for a life of voluntary poverty. As Stang once said, "This is my mission, to be poor with the poor and work with them to make a better life."[3]

A government-initiated reform effort to distribute land to the peasants was launched seven years after Sister Dorothy arrived in Brazil. Although some of the reform's supporters were motivated by humanitarian concerns, the government got behind the program for largely practical ones. Peasants who found it impossible to make a living as day laborers or tenant farmers were increasingly migrating to Brazil's cities, glutting them with tens of thousands of unemployed and encircling them with huge shanty towns and slums. The government's hope was that some of the urban congestion could be reduced if free land in the virgin Amazon rain forest was offered for the asking.

Thousands of Brazil's poor took advantage of the program, scraping together what little bit of money they could to buy a few tools and seeds before setting off into the wild. They traveled into the interior on the TA, the 3,300-mile-long Transamazon Highway that cut right through the forest. But only the first 100 miles of the road was paved. The rest was little more than a trail, hacked and bulldozed through the thick growth, sometimes rough and nearly impassable. The isolated settlements that sprang up as a result of the land reform were accessed by even rougher paths and roads branching off to the right or the left of the TA.

Peasants weren't the only Brazilians to jump on the land offer. Businessmen, politicians, and corporations laid claim to immense swaths of the rain forest. These "land sharks," as Sister Dorothy called them, often held deeds granted directly to them by government cronies. The peasants, by contrast, rarely had deeds for the land they claimed. They just presumed that any uncultivated portion they chose was automatically theirs. Inevitably, the large landowners began claiming as theirs land that peasants had settled on in good faith. "More rich came into the area," observed Sister Dorothy, "and kept taking over huge tracts of land. The people couldn't hold onto the land. There was no recourse to justice when they resisted, and the police were paid to violate the rights of those who stood up for their rights."[4] Peasant settlers were pushed deeper and deeper into the virgin forest. But as soon as they settled on new plots of land, the same landowners who had driven them off their earlier ones would claim the new as well.

The reason for this rush for land on the part of wealthy ranchers, investors, and corporations was the oldest one in the world: greed. Land in the Amazon rain forest was free and yielded huge profits. First, the virgin timber was cut and sold. Then, after this indiscriminate deforestation, the remaining undergrowth was burned off and quick-growing cattle grass sown. The denuded forest land was then used to graze thousands of heads of beef cattle whose meat would be sold on the

international market. This slash-burn-graze practice was crude and ultimately unsustainable, but it brought quick profits with virtually no over-
head. The only thing needed was easy availability of land to exploit, and
the rain forest offered a seemingly inexhaustible supply of that.

It was the growing tension between peasant settlers and land sharks
that expanded Sister Dorothy's ministry from teaching and routine parish work to activism. The Brazilian Church quickly championed the
rights of the peasants against the large landowners, and in 1975 helped
establish the Pastoral Land Commission, charged with investigating reports of harassment, intimidation, and abuse. Stang began visiting the
rain forest settlements to encourage the peasants living in them to stand
up for their rights against those who wanted to take their land. By doing
so, she angered both political authorities, who found her support of the
settlers meddlesome, and even some fellow Catholics, who believed
that nuns had no business getting involved in such matters. Her first
interrogation by the police, in fact, was prompted by a priest who
lodged an official complaint about Sister Dorothy's activities.

Over the next couple of decades, Stang became increasingly involved in defending Brazil's peasant farmers who settled in the Amazon
rain forest. She helped them organize a union to protect their claims to
their land, and she traveled hundreds of miles, often on foot, to encourage settlements to create base communities, led by laypeople, that applied Catholic social justice teachings to the conflict with large landowners. In the early 1980s, she moved to the state of Para to work with
its bishop, Edwin Krautler, an advocate of liberation theology who, like
Sister Dorothy, championed the peasants. She worked hard there building schools, establishing base communities, and helping settlers to organize.

But by the end of the decade, oppression of the poor, despite the
efforts of the Church and secular reformers, had become unbearable.
As Dorothy put it, "Our situation here in Brazil is worse each day as the
wealthy make their plans to exterminate by hunger the needy."[5] Judg-
ments like this infuriated the wealthy ranchers, who no longer saw
Sister Dorothy as merely meddlesome. She and Bishop Krautler were
both hated and feared by the economically privileged few as dangerous
threats that needed to be neutralized, and the two of them began receiving anonymous death threats. Apparently operating on the principle

that cutting off the head would kill the body as well, the ranchers decided to go after Bishop Krautler.

They hit him in 1987 as he traveled to a meeting of a farm workers' association that Stang had helped organize. The event was to be held in a forest settlement, and the bishop and an accompanying priest drove to it along a deserted road. As Dorothy described what happened, the two men had motored about fourteen miles into the forest "and were going up a steep incline [as] a truck was coming down. All of a sudden our Bishop saw the truck aim for him. . . . The steering wheel saved our Bishop, but his chest, back, mouth, [and] nose area . . . are much offended."[6] The injured bishop was flown to a hospital. His companion wasn't so fortunate. The priest traveling with Krautler died in the orchestrated collision.

Stang was shaken by the murder attempt, but she resolved to continue her work, despite the fact that a $20,000 bounty had been placed on her head. "I receive open death threats from ranchers and robbers of public lands," she wrote, "because I urge justice and friendship with the people, and I cherish their sincerity, willingness to share, hospitality, endurance, resolution and readiness. All I ask of God is his grace to help me keep on this journey."[7] Sister Dorothy knew all too well that the ranchers wanted her dead. But she wasn't backing down. "My place," she told a friend, "is here alongside these people who are constantly humiliated by others who consider themselves powerful."[8]

In the 1990s, Stang came to understand her advocacy of economic justice for the impoverished settlers as inseparably connected with advocacy for the environment. She'd seen her share of deforested tracts of the Amazon, the blackened stumps of once majestic trees still smoking from the slash-and-burn practices of the ranchers. But even she never quite appreciated the devastation until she flew over the rain forests in a small airplane and got a bird's eye view of it. She recognized then that the abuse of the small peasant farmers, who sought to cultivate and not destroy the earth, was paralleled by the wanton destruction of God's earth. Sister Dorothy concluded that to protest the one was necessarily to protest the other as well.

Her environmental ministry operated at both the national and the local level. She collaborated with other environmentalists to lobby the Brazilian government to enact legislation that protected the Amazon rain forest from rancher exploitation. They pointed out to politicians that the virgin forest was one of the world's natural wonders, that thousands of plant and animal species had already been threatened to the point of extinction by its destruction, and that the nation's beef industry could be maintained in less costly ways. But Stang, well aware that many of Brazil's political leaders were aligned with the powerful ranchers resisting environmental responsibility, also encouraged the settlers to farm in a mindfully sustainable way. They were encouraged to reforest the devastated areas, using tens of thousands of seedlings donated by concerned environmental groups around the world. Her mantra when visiting remote settlements was "cut a tree, plant a tree." Everywhere she went, she wanted both to help small farmers achieve a decent standard of living and to encourage them to respect the earth they shared with animals and plants. "How [do I] help the people recapture a relationship to Mother Earth that is tender and kind?" she constantly asked herself.[9] Her answer: "We must develop our land carefully to meet our needs with crops and farm animals, and plant seedlings to bring back the forest." She wanted to do something about the poverty endured by peasant settlers, but she also looked to the preservation of the forests so that "this beautiful universe will be here for our children."[10] She was often seen wearing a T-shirt with the slogan, "Death of the forest is the death of us all."

So far as the land sharks and cattle ranchers were concerned, Sister Dorothy's advocacy for the settlers had been bad enough. But her environmental condemnation of the slash-and-burn practices that provided cheap grazing land infuriated them. And when she appeared on national television in 2004 and began naming the worst offenders, they decided that she needed to be silenced once and for all. There had been no follow-through on the death threats that had been leveled at her over the past two decades. That was about to end. A rancher named Vitalmiro Bastos de Moura, nicknamed Bida, concocted a scheme to murder Sister Dorothy.

The setup was a dispute between Bida and a settler named Luis in the small settlement of Esperanza. Insisting that Luis's land belonged to him, Bida plowed up the crop that was planted on it and sowed cattle grass. Then he sent a few of his thugs to burn Luis and his family out of their home. Stang was called in to help Luis defend his rights, as Bida knew she would be, and he was waiting for her.

On February 11, 2005, Sister Dorothy arrived in the settlement. She was immediately threatened by some of Bida's men, who told her straight out that if she didn't leave they'd kill her. Dorothy had no intention of fleeing. She spent the night in the house of a farm union organizer, and then set out the next morning, by herself and on foot, to speak at a meeting of the local settlers. Along the road, she was accosted by two of Bida's *pistoleiros*. One of them held a revolver. Dorothy reached inside the cloth bag she always carried with her and pulled out her well-read Bible. "This is *my* weapon," she told the two men. Then she began reading the Beatitudes from the Sermon on the Mount. Halfway through, the hired assassin shot her. She fell to the ground, face down, and he emptied his gun into her back and head.

It was the rainy season, and it took the police nearly eight hours to navigate the muddy road to Esperanza. Local authorities, all in Bida's pocket, refused to move Sister Dorothy's body, and the local settlers were too frightened to do so themselves. So she lay in the rain all day. The two thugs who murdered her were eventually arrested and convicted, as was their boss Bida, following a fiery trial in which the ranch owner screamed, shockingly and ludicrously, that Sister Dorothy deserved killing because she was an American imperialist. But after serving only one year of the thirty handed down to him, Bida was released. In mid-2013, he was tried once more, and again sentenced to thirty years. It remains to be seen how long he'll stay in jail this time.[11]

The faith-inspired physical courage that Dorothy Stang displayed in standing up to the Brazilian ranchers' abuse of the peasantry and the land wasn't naïve. She'd long known that her ministry might well lead to martyrdom. Since land reform was launched in the early 1970s, nearly eight hundred advocates for settlers had been murdered. But Sister Dorothy insisted that she wasn't frightened for herself so much as "for the lives of these poor people, and if I can help them save their own lives, I will continue my work."[12]

During her funeral procession, over two thousand people, led by Bishop Krautler, accompanied Sister Dorothy on her final journey. She was buried in the Amazon region of the country she had lived in and passionately loved for so many years. As her body was lowered into its grave, one of the settlers present spoke to her. "It's all right, Sister Dorothy," he said. "We're not burying you. We're planting a seed."[13] She would've liked that.

5

ALEXANDER MEN

Christianity is a dangerous and difficult undertaking

When we hear the phrase "the age of martyrs," we typically think of Roman persecution in the early years of the Church. But in fact, more Christians were slain for their faith in the twentieth century than in all the previous ones combined. A good percentage of them fell victim to the fierce official atheism of the Soviet Union. It's impossible to know exact numbers, but most estimates put the figure somewhere between twelve and twenty million.

Alexander Men, a priest of the Russian Orthodox Church, was one of those killed in the Soviet Union because he dared to preach the gospel of Christ. But to this day, it's not entirely clear who murdered him. It might've been Soviet agents angered at his defiant evangelization. It could've been agents of the conservative wing of the Orthodox Church, upset by what they correctly saw as Father Men's dedication to ecumenical dialogue. Or, because he was born a Jew, he could've been martyred by anti-Semites. In the long run, it doesn't much matter. Whoever the perpetrators were, they silenced one of the most sensitive and far-seeing Christians of his day.

Men was born in Moscow in 1935. By that time, after nearly two decades of Soviet rule, Christianity was firmly under the iron heel of repression. Inspired by the example of Lenin, who insisted that "any flirting with a godling is the most unspeakable filth," atheism was the official position of the state.[1] The League of Militant Atheists, whose publications and meetings especially targeted young people, numbered over thirty million members. Ninety-five percent of Orthodox churches had been shut down, some of them turned into antireligious museums. All monasteries and seminaries had been closed, and thousands of bishops, monks, priests, and nuns had been executed, imprisoned, or forced into exile. A tiny fraction of the Church managed to survive publicly, but only because it declared loyalty to the Bolshevik regime. Those Christians who refused to go along with this appeasement went underground, forming what became known as the "catacomb Church."

Men was baptized and spent his formative years in this underground church. His parents were Jewish, but shortly after his birth, Men's mother converted to Christianity and received baptism along with her son. Throughout his entire childhood, Men was spiritually directed by clergy who in turn had been trained by monks of the Soviet-destroyed Optina monastery, a place famous for its tradition of holiness.

Men was a precocious student who read widely and greedily and was interested in a range of subjects. Literature, poetry, history, art, music, and religion fascinated him, but so did the sciences, particularly astronomy and biology. "From my early childhood," he recalled, "the contemplation of nature has been my *'theologia prima.'* I used to go into a forest or a museum of paleontology in the same way I went into a church. And even now, a branch with its leaves or a bird in full flight has for me more meaning than a hundred icons."[2] He initially intended, in fact, to devote himself to science. But somewhere around the age of twelve, he had a conversion experience that convinced him he was called instead to the priesthood—a risky ambition for a Soviet child in the 1940s. On his own, he began systematically studying the subjects of the underground seminary's curriculum.

Stalin died in 1953, the same year that Men graduated from high school. Blocked from a university education because of his Jewish origins, Men decided to enroll in a technical institute to study biology while he continued his covert theological studies. But after three years, his commitment to Christianity got him expelled from the institute without a degree. Taking this as a sign that henceforth he should devote himself single-mindedly to the Church, Men was ordained deacon in 1958 and priest two years later. He never lost his interest in the natural sciences, and discussions of cosmology and evolution appeared frequently in his later books, to the dismay of his more conservative Orthodox peers.

The first two years of Men's ordained life were pretty miserable. He was assigned to a parish whose rector took a dislike to him. But in 1960, after he transferred to the Moscow parish of Alabino, his life changed for the better and his ministry took off. In just a handful of years he transformed the parish into a spiritual center that attracted young and old people alike. Since the Bolshevik revolution, the few parish priests that remained at Alabino had prudently limited themselves to the celebration of the Eucharist. Men broke the mold by holding regular hours for consultation, leading Bible study groups, visiting parishioners in their homes, and encouraging the unchurched to give Christianity a try. It wasn't long before the little Alabino church became affectionately known as "the abbey," a place where God-hungry people could congregate to study, talk, and pray.

Nor was it long before Soviet officialdom took notice of Father Men. State police began searching his home periodically to ferret out forbidden books smuggled in from Europe. He was hauled to the local station on several occasions to endure long hours of interrogation. Although Men avoided overt defiance of the authorities, he learned, as all Soviet dissidents did, how to outfox them. He requested dozens of renewals of a single funeral permit, for example, in order to preside at a number of different religious services. A prolific writer from his teens, he began authoring a series of books on the history of Christianity, Jesus, and world religions that he secreted out of the country and published pseudonymously in Belgium. And he kept a cautious eye open for spies who tried to infiltrate the abbey under the pretense of religious curiosity.

After a decade at Alabino, Men was reassigned to a church outside of Moscow, probably at the insistence of the authorities. In his new parish, Novaya Derevnva, he was given a relatively free hand by the rector. (Men would remain the assistant priest at Novaya Derevnva for nineteen years, becoming its rector only the year before his death.) He continued the ministry there that he had inaugurated at Alabino, and soon had an even larger following. It became customary for Muscovites who admired him to take their summer vacations in dachas close to his parish. They would worship with him on Sundays, attend talks and lectures given by him throughout the week, and seek his spiritual guidance in private sessions. When they returned to the city after their vacations, they frequently organized independent Bible study groups that Men periodically visited.

The people most attracted to Father Men were young intellectuals who had grown up in an almost exclusively atheistic culture but who found themselves hungering for something deeper and richer. All their lives, the claim that Christianity was nonsensical superstition at best and a repressive tool of the state at worst had been drummed into them. Father Men worked hard to show them that Christianity was both smart and beautiful, concerned with social justice, and ready and willing to dialogue with and learn from alternative worldviews. He traced for them the history of Western and Eastern thought, showed the role that Christianity played, and offered instruction in the doctrines of the Faith. Just as important, he set a personal example of charity and self-giving that inspired those seekers who came to him. No matter what time of night or day, visitors were always welcome at either Men's church or the modest home, located twenty-five miles away, he shared with his wife and children. (Orthodox priests are allowed to marry.) In his efforts to reach as many people as he could, Father Men was tireless.

There were several themes central to Men's proclamation of Christianity. One was that the Faith had to speak to the world in which it was situated. As an incarnational religion, Christianity, Men taught, ought to weave itself firmly within the warp and woof of everyday life, revealing the presence of God in the most mundane tasks as well as in the most beautiful prayers and liturgies. Although appreciative of Orthodoxy's long tradition of monastic asceticism and apophatic or negative theology, Men passionately believed that this kind of otherworldliness was spiritually lopsided unless balanced by a deep appreciation for God's revelation in the material world of nature and human relationships.

Ecumenism was another of Men's passions. He insisted that there was an underlying oneness to Christianity that transcended denominational disagreements and often said that "our earthly walls of separation do not go up to heaven."[3] Men was firmly committed to the Orthodox tradition in which he had been raised and ordained, but he also celebrated the beliefs and practices of Roman Catholics and Protestants. This openness to other Christian traditions sat ill with more conservative Orthodox priests and laypersons. But Men insisted that hunkering down inside one's particular version of Christianity was more spiritual agoraphobia than denominational loyalty. "Apparently Peter the Great suffered from a psychological disorder—the fear of open spaces," he wrote. "He built himself tiny little rooms and so on. There is an illness like that—the fear of open spaces. In the history of religion, there is also this fear of open spaces."[4]

Another conviction of Men's was that Christianity, despite its two-thousand-year history, was still in its infancy. Its followers, subsequently, were still growing into the Faith step by tentative step. This accounted not only for the fragmentation of the Christian community into different sects, but also the failure of both churches and individual Christians to live according to the precepts they professed. "We are still Neanderthals in spirit and morals," wrote Men, "because the arrow of the Gospels is aimed at eternity; because the history of Christianity is only beginning. What has happened already, what we now call the history of Christianity, are the first half-clumsy, unsuccessful attempts to make it a reality."[5]

That the world has yet to fully absorb the message of Christianity is evidenced, Men believed, by the various utopianisms that have cropped up over the centuries. All humans yearn for social justice and personal completion, and this yearning is ultimately grounded in a "thirst" for "communion with the divine life."[6] The Christian message is that Jesus Christ, in his life, teachings, and Resurrection, is the source and the completion of that thirst. But in our spiritual immaturity, we frequently embrace inferior substitutions that promise us fulfillment but are unable to deliver. For Men and his contemporaries, Soviet-style communism was one of them. In stirring rhetoric, it offered individuals what their hearts most desired. But the rub, according to Men, is that the Soviet Union or any other state that makes such a promise is a false idol. Governments, no matter how benign they may be, are always "instrument[s] of coercion," and that makes them irreconcilable with genuine spiritual or material well-being, much less with Christianity, whose "good news" is "alien to coercion and to the idea of earthly autocrats."[7] At the end of the day, no materialistic ideology can enable us to realize our full potential as human beings, because materialism dehumanizes us, turning us into "merely thinking animals." Once this happens, the "doors . . . to the forces of destruction" are thrown open.[8] Just as Men's ecumenism riled conservative Orthodox Christians, so his criticisms of the communist secular state, no matter how tempered they were, angered Soviet authorities.

Even as Father Men's influence as a spiritual leader was growing, paralleling a revival of interest in Christianity throughout the Soviet Union, the government cracked down on religious expression and practice. For a brief period in the early 1960s, following Nikita Khrushchev's public denunciation of the Stalinist years of terror, there had been an easing of the official stance toward religion. But by the 1970s, with Leonid Brezhnev firmly in control of the Central Committee, repression returned. Atheism was elevated to the status of a national religion; believers were relegated to second-class citizenship and denied access to many professions, party membership, and sometimes university slots; churches were refused building permits; and couples who married in the church or had their children baptized were severely reprimanded by local workers' committees. Nor did the repression end with Brezhnev's 1982 death. If anything, his hardline successors clamped down even more firmly on religious belief over the next five years.

Despite these years of repression—or perhaps because of them—the dissident movement in the Soviet Union continued to grow. Temperamentally, Father Men wasn't one to overtly challenge the system, as peers such as Andrei Sakharov, Yelena Bonner, or Alexander Solzhenitsyn (whom Men knew) did. He preferred to continue his work of quiet but dedicated resistance by evangelizing in sermons, writings, and personal contact with the hundreds who sought him out. Even so, he was under constant surveillance by the KGB and endured regular house searches and interrogations, just as he had at his earlier parish of Alabino. But a new and ominous dimension to his persecution emerged during these years: he was attacked by the Orthodox establishment for his friendship with Roman Catholics and Protestants, and by anti-Semites for his Jewish background. Men was reviled in print from both quarters and began receiving anonymous letters that threatened his life. He ignored them, maintaining that there was too much work to be done to allow himself to be stymied by the vilification. "I work now as I have always worked," he told one concerned parishioner, "with my face into the wind." But, he admitted, "at the present time, the wind is obviously stronger."[9] Men was referring specifically to the resurgence of ultra-right and anti-Semitic groups.

And then, in the late 1980s, came the thaw of glasnost and perestroi-ka, initiated by the young and forward-looking Mikhail Gorbachev and welcomed by dissidents and Christians throughout the Soviet Union. It initiated a new spirit of openness in the hitherto locked-down society that encouraged religious expression. When the millennial anniversary of Russian Christianity was celebrated in 1988 with the full endorse-ment of the state, Men took the occasion as an opportunity to throw open his ministry. As he once said, "I have always wanted to be a Christian living not by candlelight, but in the direct light of the sun."[10] He gave hundreds of lectures and sermons, some of them televised, taught classes in Christian thought and spirituality, visited hospitals and sanatoria, something hitherto forbidden by the authorities, and began publishing a series of articles and books in his native land instead of anonymously abroad. During the final two years of his life, Men's be-came a familiar face in Russia. He lived his Christianity in the full light of day, although the anonymous threats he received grew in intensity as his ministry expanded.

Early Sunday morning on September 9, 1990, Father Men left his house to catch the commuter train to his parish in order to celebrate the liturgy. He took a shortcut to the station along a narrow path that cut through an isolated patch of birches. Not long afterward, his wife, who had remained at home, heard groaning by the front gate. She rushed outside and found Father Men, lying on the ground and covered with blood. While walking through the birches, an assailant had snuck up behind him and split the back of his skull with an axe. Men had somehow managed to make his way home before dying.

Father Men's murderer remains unknown to this day, and specula-tion about who wielded the axe is mere guesswork. Was his assassina-tion engineered by a KGB desperate to stop the mouth of one of the Soviet system's most influential religious resisters? Or was Men mur-dered by rightwing anti-Semites who, despising his ecumenism, saw him as a betrayer of Orthodoxy? The choice of an axe as the murder weapon is suggestive. In Russian tradition, the axe is a symbol of resis-tance to foreigners, and in the eighteenth and nineteenth centuries was also a popular killing instrument during pogroms. Even if the murder wasn't carried out by the ultraright, conservatives didn't hesitate to declare the act a judgment from God. As one of them wrote in a periodical, "May [Men's] death be a lesson to all those in the Church who flirt with Satanic forces."[11]

The night before his murder, Men had concluded a lecture series on the history of religions. After his death, many in the audience recalled that there was a somber tone to his words that suggested he knew his end was near. Part of what Men reminded his listeners was that it took incredible courage to be a loyal Christian. Marx, with his famous declaration that religion is the opium of the people, had presumed that the primary function of faith was to tranquilize believers. But, said Men, Christianity is not "an easy chair, a refuge, a tranquil harbor! . . . No, Christianity is not a security blanket! We must take risks in becoming Christians."[12]

Far from being an effortless jaunt down a smoothly level road, authentic Christianity, maintained Men, was more like "a mountain climbing expedition, a dangerous and difficult undertaking." Too many people who call themselves Christians prefer to stay at the bottom of the mountain, read guidebooks, and fancy that doing so is good enough. But it's not, Men said. Not by a long shot. It takes courage and resolve to reach the summit.[13]

And what can motivate and fuel this kind of courage? For Men, it wasn't simply intellectual conviction of the truth of Christianity or philosophical and theological arguments for the existence of God. Instead, it was faith as trust, "as the act of breaking through the absurdity of lifeless reality, the moment when a person says to God, 'Yes, I accept, I am listening.'"[14] Throughout his life, cut too short by the assassin's blow, Father Men had been listening to God's will and had freely accepted that following it could well lead to persecution and even death. But he recognized that what seemed a heavy burden to shoulder when looked at from one angle looked like a blessing from another. As he once said in a Holy Week sermon, "The terrible sign of the cross is at the same time a sign of joy and victory. That is why we adorn it as we do, for the cross became not only an instrument of execution, a gallows, but also the instrument of our salvation. So let us not leave our Lord alone on the Cross."[15]

6

THE TIBHIRINE MONKS

in God's face I see yours

The first thing visitors to the monastery saw was a large sign in French and Arabic that announced: Muslims Welcome for Retreats Here. For nearly a quarter century, the Cistercian or Trappist monks of Our Lady of Atlas, a monastery on the Algerian side of the Atlas mountain range, had encouraged interfaith dialogue between Muslims and Christians. Their relationship with their Muslim neighbors in the adjoining village of Tibhirine (a Berber word that means "gardens") was cordial. As one of the villagers once said to the monks, "If you go away, you will rob us of your hope, and we'll lose ours."[1]

The Tibhirine monks weren't in the business of proselytizing. Their only wish was to extend Christ's hospitality to all comers. But in March 1996, all seven of them were taken captive by the radical Armed Islamic Group (Groupe Islamique Arme, or GIA) under the pretext, as a GIA communique declared, that their presence in Tibhirine was to "draw [the Muslim villagers] away from the divine path."[2] The insurgents offered to exchange the monks for comrades of theirs who were imprisoned by Algerian authorities. After the government refused the deal, their captors cut the monks' throats one by one, severed their heads, and placed them in a public place as a warning to all Christians. When Dom Bernardo Olivera, the Abbot General of the Cistercians, flew from France to Tibhirine in May 1996 to celebrate a requiem mass for his seven slain brothers, the sign welcoming Muslims was still hanging from the wall of their empty monastery.

Our Lady of Atlas was founded in 1934 by a handful of Yugoslavian Trappists who relocated to Algeria, at that time the jewel in France's colonial crown. The largest country on the Mediterranean Sea and the second largest on the African continent, Algeria had been invaded by the French a century earlier and torn from the Ottoman Empire after a long and bloody conflict. Enticed by the French government's promise of cheap land, settlers poured into the colony and an apartheid-like class division between European newcomers and natives was quickly established.

By Our Lady's first year, French colonials—referred to as *pieds noirs* or "black feet," probably from the European-style black leather boots they wore—made up about ten percent of the Algerian population but controlled most of the nation's wealth and political power. Shortly after World War II, a twenty-seven-year war of independence erupted in Algeria, in which both the French Army and the native rebels committed horrible atrocities. France finally gave up the struggle in 1962 and Algeria became an independent Islamic republic. But internecine fighting between moderate and extremist Muslim factions continued for another forty years, with the former accepting the presence of European and Christian minorities in Algeria and the latter wanting all non-Muslims expelled from the country. The GIA was the most savage of the extremist groups. By 1994, its members were murdering a thousand people a week. Men, women and children, journalists, intellectuals, professionals, Christian clergy, and moderate Muslim imams all fell victim. The Christian presence in Algeria was reduced to just 170 clergy and 368 members of religious orders in a handful of abbeys, priories, and convents scattered throughout the country, and they were all terrified.

The first generation of monks at Our Lady of Atlas had adopted the superior attitude unfortunately all too often characteristic of colonial missionaries at the time. In their eyes, native Muslims were bizarrely exotic in their customs, heathen in their religion, and barbaric in comparison with Europeans. The founding monks were civil enough to the residents of Tibhirine, but also kept their distance from them and their monastery doors closed to them.

All that changed, however, with the 1971 arrival of Christian de Cherge, a French Trappist who was in his early thirties when he came to Our Lady. The son of an army general and descended from a long line of Parisian aristocrats, Christian initially followed in his father's military footsteps. He saw action in the Algerian war of independence, but was so disgusted by the brutality he witnessed that he resigned his commission, entered seminary, and was ordained a priest in 1964. Initially assigned to the Sacre-Coeur in Paris, a cushy assignment undoubtedly given him because of his aristocratic background, he surprised friends and family by joining the Trappists four years later. Shortly afterward he requested a transfer to Algeria.

Christian brought to Our Lady of Atlas a deep commitment to a Christianity that excluded no one. In his cell hung a photo of Gandhi with the inscription, "How can he who believes he possesses Absolute Truth truly be fraternal?" Convinced as he was that Christians and Muslims had much to teach one another about God, Christian organized semiannual gatherings that gave adherents to the two religions opportunities to discuss themes such as fraternal love, the Holy Spirit, and the multiple names of God. In these conferences, which became known as Bonds of Peace, doctrine and theology were put on hold; open-hearted speech and deep listening were the order of the day. Christian wanted to avoid the "intellectual sparring that gets in the way of getting to know one another. . . . Sharing our water, a piece of bread, a friendly handshake, says much more about what we can do together than do theological tomes."[3]

Although at first a bit wary, Christian's fellow monks soon endorsed his open-heartedness and enthusiastically elected him as their prior in 1984. With his encouragement, they worked hard to win the trust and affection of the locals and to overcome the monastery's earlier reputation for aloofness. It wasn't long before villagers and others from the area regularly visited the monastery to be treated without cost or question at the dispensary, to use the telephone or have a letter written, to fetch water from the well, or simply to relax a bit and chat. The monks, who made their living from selling honey and garden produce, also employed a few villagers as seasonal laborers. For the brothers of Our Lady, everyone who came to the monastery was welcomed, as the Rule of St. Benedict required, "as Christ."

Like their prior, all the Tibhirine monks were born in France. The oldest member, born in 1914, was Brother Luc Dochier, who had come to Our Lady in 1946. He was the monastery's cook and medical man, and he spent hours each day treating ailing or injured Muslims in the dispensary. He suffered terribly from asthma and had endured the trauma of once being kidnapped by rebels during the Algerian War. But nothing could dampen his spirits. He told his fellow monks that when his time to die came, he wanted to drink a glass of champagne while listening to a recording of Edith Piaf's "Je ne regrette rien."

Tall and thin Brother Michel Fleury, a lay brother like Luc, was born in 1944 into a working class family. Trained as a machinist, he was a member of a communist workers' union before joining the Cistercians in 1980 and transferring to Tibhirine four years later. While working with the union, he'd frequently assisted North African emigrants and had a genuine affection for them. He grieved deeply for the violence perpetrated against Muslims and Christians in the long years of war and internecine fighting. As he wrote in a 1994 letter, "We [monks] want to live here in solidarity with all the Algerians, who have already paid with their lives [and] in solidarity with all the unknown innocents."[4] A man of few words, Michel was the monastery's gardener.

Like Christian-Marie, Celestin Ringeard had served in the French army in Algeria during the war and was also a priest. Born in 1933 and ordained in 1960, he spent the first twenty-five years of his ministry as a parish priest. He entered the Trappist Order when he was fifty and arrived in Algeria three years later. Because he was a latecomer to monastic life, he sometimes found it hard to adjust to the close living arrangements in Our Lady. Christian, appreciating Celestin's need for privacy, gave him permission to take long predawn walks by himself off the monastic grounds. Endowed with considerable musical talent, Celestin served as the community's organist and cantor.

Brother Paul Favre-Miville, born in 1939, had also seen action in the French army during the Algerian War as a crack paratrooper. After his military service he returned home to work in the family plumbing business, but found himself increasingly drawn to the religious life. In 1984, he finally joined the Trappists as a lay brother and transferred to Our Lady five years later. Stocky and balding, Brother Paul was a skilled mechanic. Known among the brothers as the man with "golden hands," he was the monastery's handyman, especially responsible for the garden's irrigation system. He also served as the community hotelier. "Living the Gospels authentically," he once wrote, is "a radical challenge to all forms of totalitarianism."[5]

Brother Bruno, born Christian Lemarchand in 1930, was the son of a French army officer who took his family along with him on his various military assignments across Indochina and North Africa. Like Celestin, Bruno had been a parish priest before joining the Cistercians. He arrived at Our Lady when he was already nearly sixty years of age. With his cropped gray hair and angular, emaciated face, Bruno looked a bit like Armand de Rancé, the seventeenth-century founder of the Trappist Order. In 1992, he was named superior of Our Lady's sister house in Fes, Morocco. But he returned to Tibhirine in March 1996 for a visit just in time to be seized by the GIA.

The youngest member of the Tibhirine community, Brother Christophe Lebreton, was in many ways the most creative. Born in 1950, Christophe had worked in the city of Algiers with developmentally challenged children before coming to Our Lady in 1987. A bearded man with a bright smile, he was a skilled writer, poet, musician, and something of a mystic. He served as the monastery's novice master and subprior, and he was Christian's choice to succeed him as prior.

Beginning in late 1993, the GIA ramped up its campaign of terror to rid Algeria of Christians. After issuing a warning for all Europeans to flee the country, GIA guerrillas crept into a workers dormitory at a hydraulic plant about nine miles from Tibhirine and slit the throats of twelve Christian Croates as they slept. Many of the victims had worshipped at one time or another at Our Lady. In separate instances, four other Europeans were assassinated.

In the wake of this surge of violence, the local police chief urged the Tibhirine monks to return to France, at least until things calmed down. To remain, he warned, was "collective suicide." But Christian and his brothers resolved to stay. To pick up and leave, they worried, would baffle and hurt their neighbors, the good people of Tibhirine, who depended on them. It would also violate the spirit of radically inclusive hospitality and interfaith reconciliation that lay at the heart of the monks' ministry. As Christian saw it, he and his brothers were "at the juncture between two groups [Christians and Muslims] who are in confrontation here and, to some extent, everywhere in the West and Near East."[6] By remaining, the little community of Our Lady of Atlas hoped to extend a hand to both sides, set an example of trust, and perhaps forestall more bloodshed.

The brothers' resolve was tested just a few days later. On Christmas Eve, just as Michel had finished ringing the Angelus, three GIA guerrillas burst through the monastery gate. They rounded up the brothers at gunpoint and demanded to speak to "the pope of the house." When Christian arrived on the scene he was civil but firm. "No one has ever come with a weapon into this house of peace," he told the intruders. "Both your religion and mine forbid weapons in places of worship. If you want to talk here, you must leave your gun outside the building."[7] Either impressed or rattled by Christian's courage, the guerrillas left after stripping the monastery dispensary of medical supplies. But they warned they would be back.

The Christmas Eve visit frightened the Tibhirine monks; how could it have not? They fully understood that they were living on the edge, and this inevitably caused anxiety that revealed itself in different ways. Luc's chronic asthma worsened to such a degree that at one point he asked for last rites. Christophe and Paul found themselves struggling with sudden and uncharacteristic bouts of anger, and in their calmer moments agonized over the intensity of their desire to lash back at the guerrillas. Christian seemed not to be terribly concerned about his own fate, but he dreaded the likelihood that innocent Algerians would be blamed in the event of his or his brothers' murders. Michel despised himself for being fearful. Poor Celestin was a wreck. Jumpy and restless, terrified of the possibility of a violent death, unable to sleep or concentrate on his duties, he eventually had to give up his job as the monastery's cantor.

But for all their personal and collective anxiety, the monks of Our Lady persevered in their ministry of reconciliation. Each of them steeled himself to go about his daily affairs and to remain loyal to his prayer life. After the Christmas Eve raid, machine gun–toting GIA guerrillas occasionally showed up at the dispensary asking for medical aid. Luc, with the full approval of his brothers, extended the same hospitality to them he did to any sick visitor. "When our frères of the mountain come to see Luc," Christian wrote, "it reminds us of the need to continually practice the art of healing among all people."[8]

As the monks reflected on the danger in which they now constantly lived, a common theme began to emerge: rebirth. As Christophe wrote, "I was born again on December 24. . . . You [God] pulled me out of the grave in order to live by You, with You, and in You. . . . You say to me today: Arise, go to yourself, to your true Easter I."[9] Christian echoed the theme. "Through that experience [the Christmas Eve raid], we felt invited to be born again. The life of a man goes from birth to birth. . . . In our life there is always a child to be born: the son of God whom each of us is."[10]

Christophe's and Christian's invocation of Easter was appropriate, because they and their brothers had come to the conclusion that living in the shadow of the GIA's jihad offered the opportunity to dive ever deeper into their faith by sharing Christ's Passion. Death, they came to realize, was more than just the fate of all humans. It was also the path to resurrection. They had always accepted this as a tenet of faith. But the sword hanging over their heads helped them fully integrate it into their everyday lives. Brother Luc spoke for them all when he reflected that "there is no true love of God without an unreserved acceptance of death." For Luc and his brothers, the cultivation of love was everything. "We can only exist as humans," he wrote, "by becoming symbols of love, as manifested in Christ who, though just, submitted to injustice." Love, Luc said, should open wide, like Christ's arms on the Cross, to embrace everyone—even the devil himself.[11]

The moment that the monks had been struggling to prepare for arrived on the week leading up to Palm Sunday in 1996. Brother Bruno had just arrived at Our Lady from the Moroccan sister house to spend Easter with his brothers. Shortly after midnight on Tuesday, March 27, GIA guerrillas broke into the monastery, herded up the seven monks, and drove them into the darkness. Before they left, they ransacked the dispensary, desecrated the sanctuary, and cut the telephone line. Nearly two months later, a Moroccan radio station received a faxed communique from the GIA. "We have cut the throats of the seven monks as we said we would do. It happened this morning. May God be praised."[12]

Among the objects strewn in Christian's cell by the kidnappers was a sealed envelope with the word "Testament" written on it. The envelope was opened on May 26, Pentecost Sunday, shortly after word of the monks' murders was received. The document inside was remarkable. Christian drafted it in December 1993 and reaffirmed it in January 1994, just a week after the Christmas Eve visit from GIA guerrillas.

In his testament, Christian anticipated his own violent death at the hands of Islamist terrorists and meditated on how he wanted to meet his fate and how he hoped others would think about it. He was especially concerned to caution those he left behind not to use his murder as an occasion for blanket hatred of Algerian Muslims, who themselves often had suffered terribly at the hands of men of violence. Christian asked those who mourned him to "associate this death with so many other equally violent ones which are forgotten through indifference or anonymity."[13] He wanted no distinction made between himself and the thousands of forgotten victims of war.

Additionally, Christian refused to condemn his murderer. He wrote that at his final moment, right before the death blow, his prayer was that he would be allowed the "spiritual clarity" to beg forgiveness of God for his own sins, forgive everyone he'd ever known, "and at the same time forgive with all my heart the one who will strike me down." He also prayed that he would have time to thank God for the life he'd led, and then to thank his unknown assailant. "And also you, my last-minute friend, who will not have known what you are doing: Yes, I want this THANK YOU and this A-DIEU to be for you too, because in God's face I see yours."[14] Brother Christophe, in notes written at Easter the year before, had said something similar. In thinking about what it meant to live at Our Lady of Atlas and to serve the people of Tibhirine, he wrote: "We [monks] have this theme: You [God] on the face of all the living."[15]

At the requiem mass for the slain Tibhirine monks, Dom Bernardo, the head of their order, praised them for remaining true to their ministry. It takes great courage to love, he reminded those gathered, because love requires us to give ourselves to others who may seem alien and threatening. But, said Dom Bernardo, "we must enter into the world of the other, whether that person be Christian or Muslim. In fact, if the 'other' does not exist as such, there is no space for true love. We need to be disturbed and enriched by the existence of the other. Let us remain open and sensitive to every voice that challenges us. Let us choose love, forgiveness, and communion against every form of hatred, vengeance, and violence."[16]

Brothers Christian, Luc, Michele, Celestin, Paul, Bruno, and Christophe did precisely that.

7

MYCHAL JUDGE

you do it with the grace of God

He delivered his final sermon on September 10, 2001, the day before he died. It was at a memorial mass in a Bronx fire station, commemorating a captain who had sacrificed himself in a horrendous fire six years earlier to shove two men under his command to safety.

In his homily, Father Mychal Judge, beloved chaplain to the New York City Fire Department (FDNY), spoke of the fragility of life and the courage of the men and women who put themselves on the line to rescue others. "You do what God has called you to do," he told the firefighters. "You show up. You put one foot in front of another. You get on the rig and you go out and you do the job. . . . No matter how big the call. No matter how small. You have no idea what God is calling you to. But he needs you. He needs me. He needs all of us."[1]

The following morning, when the first plane hit the North Tower, Judge and hundreds of firefighters, cops, and emergency personnel loaded onto their rigs and went to where God needed them. Soon afterward, he was dead, struck by falling debris. Judge's was the first officially recorded death on that terrible day. The photograph of dust- and soot-covered firemen carrying away his dead body in a chair jerry-rigged as a stretcher has become an iconic reminder of the tragedy of 9/11.

It's also a reminder of the kind of physical courage that Christian faith can inspire and sustain. Once, in speaking about Maximilian Kolbe, the priest who sacrificed himself to save a fellow Auschwitz prisoner, Judge remarked that when presented with a challenge, one can back away or go forward. If the latter, a "great and wonderful thing will happen. It takes courage in the midst of fear, and you do it with the grace of God."[2] Grace gave Kolbe the courage to take the place of a man earmarked for death by the Nazis, and grace gave Mychal Judge the courage to walk into an inferno in the hope of helping the people trapped in it.

Judge had wrestled with challenges from an early age. Born in Brooklyn in 1933 to Irish immigrant parents, he lost his father when he was only six years old. He felt the loss for the rest of his days, often remarking to friends that he didn't fear death because at last he would be reunited with his father. The boy soon took on odd jobs—delivering groceries, shining shoes—to help out his widowed mother and two siblings. Befriended by a Franciscan friar, who most likely was a father figure for the boy, it wasn't long before young Mychal decided that he wanted to join the order himself. He entered seminary when he was fifteen, was received by the Franciscans six years later, and was ordained a priest in 1961.

For thirteen years following his ordination, he served two different New Jersey parishes. He was devoted to his congregations at both places and they to him, although his championship of civil rights for black Americans riled some of his more conservative parishioners. In 1976, he began a three-year stint as assistant to the president of Siena College, a Franciscan institution in New York. He then returned to New Jersey to resume parish ministry, taking a sabbatical year in 1984 to study in Canterbury, England. In 1986 he transferred back to his beloved New York City to join the staff at St. Francis of Assisi Church in mid-Manhattan, a place famous for its ministry to the homeless and down-and-out. It was the same church in which the Franciscan who had helped Judge discover his vocation years earlier had served.

The wound of losing his father created a loneliness in Judge that was never quite filled. In seminary, separated from his mother and siblings, the loneliness reached a point where he began to drink, sneaking unconsecrated wine from the sacristy whenever he could. After he was priested and assigned to parish work, the drinking continued, reaching a high point during his time at Siena College. Although he never showed any of the signs and was suspected by none of his acquaintances, Judge recognized that he was an alcoholic. He attended his first AA meeting in 1978 and remained sober for the rest of his life. More than once, he publicly admitted that staying off the booze was hard. But he never wavered in his resolve to do so.

What Judge wasn't so willing to speak openly about was his sexuality. Part of the pain that his drinking anesthetized was the realization that he was a homosexual. For years, the knowledge of his orientation tortured him. The church in which he was a priest, after all, condemned homosexuality as a sin, and for a long time a self-loathing Judge accepted that judgment. Although he remained celibate his entire life, by the 1980s he had made peace with his sexuality. But he was reluctant to speak publicly about it, and once told a friend that he definitely didn't want the firefighters to whom he ministered to know he was gay. They had enough to worry about, he said, without having to wrap their minds around the idea of a homosexual chaplain. Judge didn't particularly approve of the macho ethos of New York City firefighters, but he respected the importance of what they did too much to risk discombobulating them in any way.

Judge's friends and acquaintances were unanimous on two points: he came into his own when he returned to his beloved New York City in 1986, and he was the most generous person they knew. Judge loved the city as only a native can, and he delighted in taking long walks down its streets and avenues. At least once a week he walked to the Brooklyn Bridge to gaze upon the Manhattan skyline. He seemed to know everyone he met, and everyone knew him. More than one friend fondly called him a "prince of the city" and observed that he soaked up energy from the hustle and bustle of the Big Apple.

As a Franciscan, Judge's vows committed him to a life of voluntary poverty. But his temperamental dislike of ownership was intense, even for a follower of Francis of Assisi. He refused to have a bank account, the only money he tended to carry were dollar bills that he handed out to the homeless and indigent, and he gave away (sometimes to the annoyance of his benefactors) any gift of clothing he received to people in the streets who needed it more than he did. Shortly before his death, he packed up the few books he owned and mailed them to a friend. He was simply selfless when it came to ownership—with one exception. After he became a FDNY chaplain, he was given a car that he absolutely adored. Sometimes he drove it through the city with light flashing and siren blaring for the sheer fun of it. But as one of his fellow friars observed, it wasn't the actual automobile that Judge prized—he didn't even know its make—but the fact that he could use it to transport goods to folks who needed them. The backseat was always crammed with water bottles, blankets, over-the-counter medicines, and food that Judge dispensed to the indigent.

Judge was just as generous with his time as his material possessions. He spent a good deal of it in prayer, on his knees first thing in the morning and visiting the friary's chapel last thing at night—he would typically tell his brother Franciscans that it was time to "say good night to the boss"—but otherwise he was always on the go, visiting patients and shut-ins, transporting the homeless to clinics or hustling to get them into shelters, walking the streets on the lookout for runaways who needed help, finding treatment for addicts and alcoholics. Back in the friary at the end of a long and exhausting day, he'd spend hours on the telephone returning calls that had piled up during his absence. Anyone who needed him got his full attention. A friend remembered that once when he and Judge were approached by a homeless man who asked for a dollar or two, Judge instead took him to a nearby Burger King and engaged him in conversation while he ate. Nor was it a pious put-on. Judge was genuinely interested in him and his story.

The first cases of a mysterious new disease, soon to be called AIDS, began cropping up in New York City in the 1980s. Little was known about it, including how it was contracted, except that it seemed to affect gay men disproportionately. Medical personnel, like the general public, were frightened, and many of them avoided personal contact with patients suffering from it. It wasn't uncommon in those days for the victims of the new disease to be quarantined in hospitals, with masked and gloved nurses and assistants refusing to come close enough to bathe or feed them. Father Mychal immediately felt called to minister to AIDS patients—he considered them the modern-day analog of St. Francis's lepers—and began to make the rounds of hospitals, hospices, and private homes to offer them spiritual comfort. He also mobilized committees to raise money, supplies, and resources for their physical comfort. It wasn't uncommon for gay patients, on first encountering a man wearing the Franciscan habit, to rage at him for the moral censure they'd received from the Catholic Church. But with few exceptions, Judge's empathy and tender care won them over. He refused to preach at them, much less to judge them. Most often, when he visited a new patient, he simply massaged his feet and sat with him awhile.

His ministry to gay people continued even after the 1986 Vatican's *On the Pastoral Care of Homosexual Persons* declared that homosexuals exhibited "a strong tendency toward an intrinsic moral evil," and that homosexuality was an "objective disorder."[3] Immediately following its publication, the New York Chancery forbade Catholic churches to host meetings of Dignity, the organization of Christian gays and lesbians. Judge ignored the prohibition and continued to celebrate mass for Dignity members for the rest of his life. "Is there so much love in the world," he once asked, "that we can afford to discriminate against any kind of love?"[4]

The depth of Father Mychal's compassion and generosity was revealed in July 1996 when TWA Flight 800 exploded and crashed into the Atlantic Ocean twelve miles after taking off from John F. Kennedy Airport. All 230 passengers and crew members perished. Survivors of the victims congregated at a Ramada Hotel near JFK as search teams dredged up wreckage and bodies. For over two weeks, Judge drove back and forth between Manhattan and Queens to spend twelve hours a day with them. He held nightly masses, attended by both Catholics and non-Catholics, regularly met with, counseled, and consoled family members shattered by grief, and in general made himself as available to the survivors as possible. His compassion for them came through in one of his homilies. "God is present," he told the mourning friends and relatives, "loving, smiling, having received our loved ones. They are in his presence, illumined by his smile and warmed by his love. His kingdom is enriched this day, so enriched, by many beautiful souls. . . . Our world is so empty without them. . . .We live our sorrow together. . . . Fill us with courage, we ask You. We beg You."[5]

Families of loved ones who perished on Flight 800 remembered Father Mychal with great fondness and gratitude. Years later, New York mayor Rudy Giuliani spoke for all of them. "There is no way to exaggerate [Judge's] ability to understand people and get into their hearts and minds," he said. "Flight 800, that was like a marathon. It was in many ways a prelude to the World Trade Center."[6]

Judge's own wounds—the loneliness he had suffered since the death of his father, his addiction to drink, guilt over his sexuality—made him a better priest than he might otherwise have been. They encouraged the empathy and deep compassion that enabled him to relate so effectively to people suffering from grief, homelessness, addiction, illness, and hopeless despair. He brought these wounds, and the gifts they birthed, with him to the New York City Fire Department when he became a chaplain in 1992.

The chief duty of a FDNY chaplain is to minister to the firefighters in the units to which he's assigned. As a chaplain, Judge officiated at weddings for firefighters, baptized their children, and occasionally buried men killed in the line of action. He celebrated mass regularly at their station houses, and often shared their meals and slept over in their living quarters. He also counseled firefighters who, because of the toll their work took on them, often suffered from depression or addiction problems. Like all fire chaplains, Judge also rode the rig when calls came in, making himself available to both the victims of fire and to firefighters who might be physically or emotionally overwhelmed by the blaze.

Being a fire department chaplain required a certain amount of physical courage, but Father Mychal had demonstrated as far back as 1974 that he had it in abundance. While serving one of his New Jersey parishes, he heard about a nearby hostage situation. A distraught man had held his wife and two children at gunpoint for over twelve hours, and the cops and emergency crew personnel surrounding his house were unable to break the standoff. Judge arrived on the scene, had himself hoisted by a fire engine ladder to a second floor window of the hostage-taker's home, and began talking to him. Onlookers didn't know which to expect first: Judge losing his precarious perch on the ladder and plummeting to earth, or the hostage taker shooting him. But against all odds, Judge succeeded in convincing the man to surrender.

He displayed the same kind of courage on the morning of 9/11. He was at the Manhattan friary when a fellow Franciscan burst into his room and shouted that a plane had just crashed into the North Tower at the World Trade Center. Judge immediately grabbed his heat-resistant coat and helmet and caught a ride down to the site with Captain Danny Brethel of the Engine 1/Ladder 24 House. Both men would soon lose their lives.

The scene was nightmarish. By the time they arrived, the second plane had hit the South Tower and both skyscrapers were burning badly. Fire chiefs and crew on the ground were scrambling to find ways to get people down from the upper floors, but the huge fireballs that exploded when the two planes hit had cut off access. Rudy Giuliani, the city's mayor, was on the scene, but he seemed just as bewildered as everyone else by what was happening. At one point he asked Judge, whom he knew, to pray for the firefighters and the victims. A bit later, he told the priest that he should leave because the situation was too dangerous. Judge replied that his place was with the firefighters, emergency personnel, and cops.

People trapped in the towers' upper floors began to jump, preferring quick death after a nine-second fall to an agonizing one by fire. Some of them hit emergency crew members on the ground, killing them instantly. Several of the jumpers landed not far from where Judge was standing, next to a blown-out window in the North Tower's lobby. Fire chiefs bellowed though bullhorns for their guys to get off the sidewalk.

Judge, like so many others, seemed dazed by what was going on. Firefighters who knew him later recalled that they'd never seen him looking so grim. He made no eye contact with them as they scurried past him, something unusual for the friendly priest. Instead, he seemed to be gazing into the distance, unable to focus.

Part of the reason for his apparent detachment was undoubtedly shock. But it's also clear that during his final moments, Father Mychal was deep in prayer. It so happened that a French cinema director, Jules Naudet, was at the Trade Center that morning to make a documentary. He kept his camera rolling after the planes hit, and caught Judge on film, his mouth visibly moving in prayer. Firemen later remembered what he was praying: "Please, God, end this now!"[7] In the midst of his prayers, Judge ministered to the fallen firefighters as best he could, giving those who needed them last rites.

It's not clear exactly when or how he died, but it couldn't have been long after Naudet captured him on film. Judge apparently had taken off his fire helmet, perhaps as he knelt to give last rites, just as the South Tower, which had been hit by the second plane, came crashing down. The collapse shot debris into the lobby of the North Tower, and some of it caught Father Mychal in the back of the head. There was no visible wound when his body was found. Some of the emergency personnel he had loved and served so well carried it away from the tower; many who afterward saw the photograph of them were struck by how closely the image resembled a pieta. A young fireman and a cop said a couple of prayers over Judge's body and laid it on the altar of a nearby church.

In an interview recorded a few months before 9/11, an unusually sober Judge had reflected on his own death. "I wonder," he mused, "when my last half hour's gonna be. Will it be doing something for someone, trying to save a life?"[8] As things turned out, that was exactly how Judge's last half hour was spent. The grace that had sustained him through all his challenges by enabling him to face them with courage and fidelity to duty literally lasted to his final breath. And that was exactly as it should have been. As one of Judge's friends put it, "This is how he would've scripted the end."[9]

When a British priest friend of Father Mychal received word of his death, he said: "Heroic virtue was demonstrated by Mychal on that day in a way that redeems the evil of the event itself."[10] But Judge would've thought that too strong a statement. It was the cops, firemen, and EMT guys, he would've insisted, not he, who were the heroes. He was only doing what he had been called to throughout his forty years of ordained life: "To be today," as he once said, "to be this moment, to keep the gospel message, bring hope and life, to preach and renew."[11]

Part II

Moral Courage

8

RUTH MANORAMA

the Church should speak out firmly

A caste system based solely upon the accident of birth has segregated India's population for centuries. Although its original intent was apparently to classify people according to their social function—priests and academics, soldiers and guards, landowners and merchants, and farmers and peasants—it in fact established a stratification in which privilege and opportunity is determined by one's place in the social pecking order, and in which mobility is impossible. At the very bottom of the hierarchical pyramid is the "outcast" caste—the Dalits, traditionally known as the "untouchables." They make up a little over sixteen percent of India's huge population.

Caste discrimination was outlawed by the 1947 Indian constitution, and an affirmative action program was launched to improve the social and economic conditions of the Dalits. There's been a little improvement in their lot, and a Dalit was actually elected president of India in the mid-1990s, something unthinkable in earlier periods. But the law is one thing and deeply engrained cultural prejudice that hinders its implementation is another. To this day, Dalits for the most part remain the least privileged group of people in India. Members of higher castes, especially in the rural areas, refuse to eat or socialize with them or live in the same neighborhoods. Dalit schoolchildren are often required to sit apart from other students and their parents are expected to queue in separate lines at polling booths. Restaurants and grocery stores frequently refuse Dalits service, many postal carriers refuse to deliver their mail, and villages often block their access to communal water sources.

The most distasteful jobs in Indian society are reserved for Dalits. They include unskilled manual labor of all kinds, but especially latrine and sewer cleaning and street sweeping. Even when Dalits succeed in getting better jobs, their wages are likely to be less than the national norm, and the wealth gap between them and the rest of Indian society, already huge, is steadily widening. The Dalits' harsh living conditions make for a life expectancy that's four years shorter than that of higher caste members. They have a high infant mortality and illiteracy rate. Every eighteen minutes a Dalit becomes a crime victim, and many of the outrages inflicted on them go uninvestigated and unpunished by indifferent law enforcement officers.

About seventy percent of India's Dalits are Christian. Christianity is India's third largest religion after Hinduism and Islam. That sounds impressive until the raw numbers are examined. Compared to over 800 million Hindus and nearly 150 million Muslims, there are barely 24 million Indian Christians, making them a relatively tiny religious minority often discriminated against by both Hindus and Muslims. The millions of Dalits who are also Christian thus endure a double discrimination, and not simply from non-Christians. Higher caste Christian clergy and laity often succumb to the same caste prejudice as their non-Christian countrymen.

At the very bottom of the caste order, are Dalit Christian women. In addition to enduring the poverty and contempt caste and religious prejudices breed, they face gender discrimination. Frequently forced to take the unsanitary and dangerous jobs that even Dalit men won't accept, while at the same time struggling to hold their families together, Dalit women wear out quickly and die young. Many of them are forced into prostitution, either on the streets or in the temples. Violence against them, especially sexual violence, is staggering.[1]

Ruth Manorama has championed Dalit women, the "Dalits of the Dalits" as she calls them, for over three decades. Born into a Dalit family, she knows from firsthand experience what it's like to be an economic and gender outcast in Indian society. As a Christian, she's also all too familiar with religious bigotry. But her commitment to Christ's message of love and compassion gives her the moral courage to defend the rights of Dalit women and to buck the overwhelming tide of

RUTH MANORAMA

Indian prejudice against Dalits in general. Her outspokenness on behalf of India's marginalized is a bold challenge to her culture's status quo.

Manorama was born in 1952 in Tamil Nadu, a state in the southeastern tip of the Indian subcontinent. The Dalit population is large there. In fact, Tamil Nadu has the fourth largest percentage of Dalits of all the Indian states. Most are concentrated in the capital city of Chennai, where Manorama was raised. Manorama's childhood home was a training ground for her work as an adult. "I grew up in a fairly progressive atmosphere with Christian values where you gave freely and treated people with respect."[2] She remembers her parents as always ready to extend a helping hand to anyone in need of a meal or help in filling out an official form. The lesson she took away from their example was that she had an obligation to serve the poor just as Christ did.

Manorama's initial plan was to train as a physician so that she could offer medical aid to the woefully under-cared-for Dalit community of Chennai. She attended the city's Women's Christian University and earned a degree in science. But during her university years she did a lot of volunteer work in city slums and outlying poverty-stricken villages and gradually discovered that her heart was in working to better the economic and social status of Dalits rather than in medicine. So after completing her undergraduate studies she went on to earn another degree in social work at the University of Madras. That was in 1975.

As a social worker, Manorama soon concluded that culturally sanctioned discrimination against the Dalits was so widespread that the only way to counteract it was to organize on the regional and national levels. Efforts on behalf of individual Dalits and their families remained important to her, but it was dishearteningly obvious that whatever help she managed to get them was likely to evaporate in the hostile environment in which they lived. So beginning in the early 1980s, Manorama began to work on two related fronts. The first was to build a national coalition to defend the legal and economic rights of Dalits in general and Dalit women in particular. The second was to reform those Indian Christian churches which shared the national prejudice against Dalits, apparently forgetful of St. Paul's observation, "There is neither Jew nor Gentile, neither slave nor free, nor is there male and female, for you are all one in Christ Jesus" (Gal 3:28).

In taking on these two tasks, Manorama drew strength from three sources. First and foremost, she sought to emulate the example of Jesus. "I am Christian and Jesus is my inspiration," she said in a 2006 interview. "He taught us equality, peace and justice."[3] For Manorama, an essential part of her faith is laboring to help build the upside-down kingdom inaugurated and proclaimed by Jesus in which the first are last and the last first. Jesus ministered to the Dalits of his day who were also scorned by "respectable" members of society. His love for the marginalized translated into an embrace of them in the face of popular scorn and public discrimination. He befriended them, healed them, ate with them, listened to them, and eventually died for them. His moral courage is Manorama's ideal, and it gives her the will to continue despite the sometimes furious censure of non-Dalit Indians.

But moral courage, essential as it is, needs to be supplemented with tactical savvy when it comes to organizing for large-scale reform. So Manorama's second source of strength comes from social activists Saul Alinsky and Paulo Freire. From the American Alinsky, she learned the importance of openly challenging entrenched institutional inequality and bigoted popular opinion in order to generate a public debate. The first step in resisting injustice is to bring it out into the open, exposing it so that its ugly reality simply can't be denied. The Brazilian Freire taught her the importance of helping an oppressed people become more conscious of the power they possess to improve their own condition. Manorama was exposed to the thought of both men in the mid-1980s while participating in a cross-cultural study that compared the condition of black American women and Indian Dalit women. But her own radicalism stops short of the violence that the secular Marxist Alinsky sometimes advocated or at least declined to condemn. Her approach as a Christian is to adapt the organizational tactics of liberation movements to the pacifism preached, practiced, and commanded by Jesus.

A third major source of strength for Manorama is the work of Tamil novelist Bama Faustina Soosairaj, who goes simply by "Bama." A contemporary of Manorama's and a fellow Dalit, Bama was also raised in a Christian family and actually spent nearly a decade as a Roman Catholic nun before leaving to devote herself to writing. Her novels, semiautobiographical accounts of Dalit life in southeastern India, are unflinchingly honest portrayals of the hardships endured by Dalits, especially women. But they also applaud the patient, faith-fed resilience of Christian Dalits and their efforts to make the most of their situation. Manorama especially likes a passage from Bama's 1994 novel *Sangati* that describes the resolve of the protagonist, a Dalit woman: "To bounce like a ball that has been hit became my deepest desire, and not to curl up and collapse because of the blow."[4] The nonviolent resistance recommended in this passage lies at the heart of Manorama's tactical style of opposing popular discrimination against Dalits. Like a person skilled in jujitsu, her method is to catch her opponent off guard by refusing to duplicate his violence in word or deed, and then to take advantage, nonviolently, of his surprise.

Manorama's large-scale organizing got off the ground in the mid-1980s when she served as the general secretary of Women's Voice, an activist group dedicated to empowering Dalit women, and the Christian Dalit Liberation Movement, set up specifically to lobby on behalf of the huge Dalit Christian community.

In her leadership of Women's Voice and, later, of the National Federation of Dalit Women, Manorama has led the nationwide struggle against the eviction of women from slum tenements that land developers want to raze. She also has worked to establish trade unions and a minimum wage for women domestic workers. Her aim throughout has been to provide some degree of autonomy and security for Dalit women in a nation dominated by caste and males. Her constituency, she says, traditionally "are vulnerable and dependent on male partners who make all the decisions. Although it looks as if women are progressing on many fronts, in terms of power relations, it is still unequal. Our law application is unequal and our laws are patriarchal." To change those laws requires a grassroots power base strong enough to influence political decisions. But Manorama is clear that her effort to empower Dalit women has a goal that transcends politics. "I am not talking of politics for making money," she insists. "Our struggle is not for garnering wealth but for reclamation of the human spirit."[5] As important as it is to improve the material conditions of Dalit women, Manorama recognizes that public acknowledgment of their dignity as human beings and children of God is also crucial. In its absence, the caste system that relegates them to the status of societal dregs endures. Even worse, Dalit women, despite their abilities and talents, internalize the disdain in which they're held.

In her leadership of the Christian Dalit Liberation Movement, Manorama has taken on a campaign especially important to her as a Christian woman: nudging Indian Christian communities away from their own allegiance to the caste system. The very fact that this is a necessary task is tragically ironic for at least two reasons.

The first is that English-speaking missionaries made a lot of progress in the nineteenth and early twentieth centuries toward undermining India's caste system. As Manorama sees it, they were guided by a "philosophy of love and justice" that saw all as equal in the eyes of God and mandated special concern for the poor, the homeless, the sick, and the despised. This naturally led them to embrace Dalits as their brothers and sisters and to encourage native Indians who converted to Christianity to do likewise.

Moreover, tens of thousands of Dalits converted when they realized that the Christian faith welcomed them as sons and daughters of God rather than rejecting them as "untouchables." They believed they had found a community in which love, rather than caste, was the ruling principle. And for many years, this belief was more or less justified.

But gradually, Manorama argues, traditional caste distinctions began to creep back into the churches. After Indian independence, when high caste churchmen filled the vacuum left by departing English missionaries, the same kind of discrimination against Dalits that characterizes the Indian culture at large became noticeable in the Christian community. Since then, "the Church in large part has remained within the control of the upper castes," and this means that Dalit Christians, particularly the women, are looked down upon. The aim of Manorama's Christian Dalit Liberation Movement is "to revolutionize the Church and reaffirm its missionary zeal which has always been present in service and justice, not just for the rich but also for the poor."[6]

Manorama is confident that the "love of Jesus" can overcome the blight of caste thinking in the Christian community. There are plenty of Christians who exemplify this love in their lives—she's especially impressed by the nuns, like Mother Teresa's Missionaries of Charity, who devote their entire lives to urban and rural Dalits—and she believes that their spirit of openness can convert the entire Church. It also helps that in recent years thousands of Dalits have been ordained as priests and pastors, and their presence within the Indian churches is helping to erode the remnants of caste mentality. These "idealistic pastors," by "demanding radical and more equitable approaches from within the Church itself," are shaking things up for the better.[7]

Helping the Church heal from "the scourge of caste" is essential for its internal spiritual health, and that in turn is a necessary condition for the Church recapturing its sense of mission to the wider community. Jesus came to minister to the marginalized and dispossessed, and the Church which acts in his name—which claims, in fact, to be a continuation of his very ministry—is called to do the same. So Christian leaders in India "need to stand up and talk the truth and speak out firmly" about the way the nation treats Dalits. But instead of doing that, "the Church that ought to be providing the necessary shield and umbrella is being defensive." Manorama is working to change that. "It's time for the Church to stand up," she insists, and her hope is to help it do exactly that.[8]

In 2006, Manorama's courageous efforts on behalf of Dalit women were recognized when she was honored with a Right Livelihood Award, known as the "alternative Nobel Peace Prize." In her acceptance speech, she reiterated her core belief that reform must aim at a spiritual as well as a material rejuvenation. "Dalit women," she said, "believe in promoting a massive cultural movement to cleanse the minds of people of caste notions and implant in its place the attitude of liberty, equality and fraternity."[9] But given her Christian faith, Manorama could also have said that the mass movement of Dalit women of which she is a leader promotes a cleansing of the soul as well.

9

SHAHBAZ BHATTI

as a follower of Christ, my destiny is to speak up.

Pakistan isn't a Christian-friendly nation. Ninety-six percent of its 190 million people are Muslim. Pakistan, in fact, has the second-largest concentration of Muslims in the entire world. Christians account for a tiny 1.5 percent of its population.

But the sheer preponderance of Muslims isn't what makes the country a dangerous place for Christians. For the first forty years of its existence, Pakistan, even though officially a Muslim state, was largely secular in both public policy and pronouncement, with very few instances of religious violence. This was thanks to the efforts of Muhammad Jinnah, the nation's founder. Mindful of the endless bickering between India's Muslims and Hindus, he advocated for a religiously tolerant Pakistan constitution. "Pakistan is not going to be a theocratic State to be ruled by priests with a divine mission," he promised in 1948, shortly before he died. "We have many non-Muslims—Hindus, Christians, and Parsis—but they are all Pakistanis. They will enjoy the same rights and privileges as any other citizens and will play their rightful part in the affairs of Pakistan."[1] For several years, it appeared as if Jinnah's vision would become a reality.

The trouble began in the mid-1980s with the introduction of a set of blasphemy laws that criminalized actions and speech deemed insulting to Islam, the Qur'an, or the prophet Muhammad, and prescribed unbelievably stiff penalties ranging from imprisonment to execution. The laws, some of the most repressive in the world, were inconsistent with both Pakistan's constitutionally guaranteed freedom of religion and the 1948 Universal Declaration of Human Rights, of which Pakistan was a signatory. But the laws' architect, the dictator General Zia ul-Haq, pushed for their adoption to curry favor with Muslim critics of the liberal democracy of his predecessor, Zulfikar Ali Bhutto.

Predictably, the laws opened the door to egregious and repeated abuse. Designed, according to Zia and the clerics who championed them, to protect the integrity of Islam, they almost immediately became weapons for religious bigots to wield at will against vulnerable religious minorities, especially Pakistan's handful of Christians. Hundreds of complaints against Christians have been lodged under the blasphemy laws, almost always under the thinnest pretense. The very existence of the laws creates a climate of intolerance that gives Muslims license to act on personal grudges or feuds and encourages fanatics to attack anyone they consider an infidel. Alongside the official persecution, street "justice," implicitly sanctioned by the state, is commonplace. Scores of victims, Muslim as well as Christian, have been savagely beaten and even murdered by zealous gangs acting in the name of religion.

One of the worst atrocities spawned by Pakistan's religious repressiveness was the August 2009 massacre in the Punjab town of Gojra. A rumor spread among local Muslims that during a Christian wedding, the guests had cut up a copy of the Qur'an and used the pieces as confetti. The story, as it turned out, was utterly false. But a furious town council immediately convened to accuse the wedding host of blasphemy, and before the day was out Muslim thugs, many of them bused in from surrounding villages, torched forty Christian households and four churches. Ten Christians were killed while local constables stood passively watching. Eight of the victims, including four women and a child, died in the flames. Archbishop of Canterbury Rowan Williams spoke for millions around the world when he denounced the rampage as "an outrage against common humanity" that deserved "forthright condemnation."[2] Although Pakistan prosecutors went through the motions of arresting and trying some seventy perpetrators, all were acquitted because terrified Gojra Christians refused to testify against them. Afterward, one of the defendants crowed, "There are no witnesses because they [the Christians] know that they are wrong. We got justice. Even though none of us did it, Christians still deserve it, because they are blasphemers."[3]

A year after angry Muslims took the blasphemy laws into their own hands at Gojra, another instance of religious repression, also in Punjab province, shocked the international community. A twenty-eight-year-old Christian farmworker named Aasia Bibi had been ordered to fetch drinking water for her fellow field hands, all of whom happened to be Muslims. They refused the water when she arrived with it, claiming that it was unclean because it was offered by an infidel. Heated words were exchanged, during which Muslims claimed that Bibi insulted the Prophet. News of what happened spread quickly, and later that day a furious mob attacked her and her family. Police arrived just in time to keep her from being beaten to death. But instead of arresting her assailants, they seized Bibi, charging her with a violation of the blasphemy laws. After a year in jail, the mother of five was finally tried, and in November 2010, incredibly, she was found guilty and sentenced to death. Not yet executed, almost certainly because of international outcry, she remains in prison.

After Bibi's verdict was announced, Salmann Taseer, the governor of Punjab, decided that things had gone too far in his province. Recoiling from the religious bigotry that sparked both her death sentence and the murders at Gojra, he visited Bibi in prison and publicly denounced the blasphemy laws under which she had been sentenced. Just a few weeks later, Taseer was gunned down by one of his own bodyguards, who afterward said the attack was retribution for the governor's defense of a blasphemer. The guard became a hero overnight. Whenever he appeared in public for court appearances, he was showered with rose petals as ecstatic onlookers rushed to embrace him. Thousands of Pakistanis loudly demanded his release. Even some who were noted for their liberalism bowed to public pressure and applauded his murderous act. Muslim clerics warned the faithful against mourning Taseer or attending his funeral.

As things turned out, it was one of the country's few Christians who organized a memorial service for Taseer. Shahbaz Bhatti, a Roman Catholic from the city of Lahore, dared to publicly stand against the popular tide by not only honoring the slain governor but applauding his condemnation of the blasphemy laws. When Bhatti was also assassinated just a few weeks after Taseer, it surprised few people. His opposition to the blasphemy laws for a good half of his life made him a likely target of Pakistani Islamicists.

As a devout Christian, Bhatti was in a good place to observe how the blasphemy laws and the hostile climate they bred had damaged his fellow religionists. In addition to dangling the perpetually menacing sword of official persecution over Christians, the laws also provided unofficial but very real permission to discriminate against them. Christians were typically relegated to menial jobs in which they were paid low wages and treated with contempt. The field hands who worked alongside Aasia Bibi weren't alone in their refusal to touch food or drink prepared by Christians. Many Pakistani Muslims regularly boycott restaurants and cafes that employ Christian cooks or servers. Additionally, Christians are barred from the highest offices of the land, and they are underrepresented in the judiciary, senate, national assembly, and military officer corps. They are in every sense of the word second, if not third, class citizens.

While he was still a student, Bhatti determined to do something about the official and unofficial discrimination endured by Pakistani Christians. Inspired by his father—a devout teacher who once told his son, "I devoted you for this cause, for the Christian rights. And you should stand to give witness"[4] —in 1985 Bhatti helped create the Christian Liberation Front, an organization that lobbied for better treatment of Pakistani Christians. Nine years later, as head of the All Pakistan Minorities Alliance, he coordinated a nationwide campaign against the blasphemy laws. In 2002, he formally joined the Pakistan People's Party (PPP), the progressive democratic political party founded by Bhutto in 1967. Already under suspicion for his advocacy of the civil rights of Christians and other religious minorities, his left-of-center politics earned him government surveillance. His name was added to a no-flight list of officially designated troublemakers forbidden to leave the country.

By 2008, Bhatti had become the public face of resistance to the blasphemy laws, which he typically referred to as "tools of victimization." His concern wasn't only for persecuted Christians. Bhatti spoke out in defense of Hindus, Shiites (about a quarter of the nation's Muslims), and other religious minorities. Partly in the hope of co-opting him and thereby toning down his criticisms, partly as a strategy to appear less repressive to the international community, the Pakistani government appointed Bhatti to a newly created cabinet position, federal minister for minorities affairs, in 2008. In taking the oath of office, he was clear about his intention to advocate for all religious minorities in Pakistan, promising to "speed up efforts to promote unity and understanding [and] to tackle the issues of intolerance, hatred, prejudice, and violence." But he also openly confessed that his Christian faith was the bedrock on which he would stand to perform his duties as the national advocate for religious minorities. "Jesus is the nucleus of my life," he said, "and I want to be his true follower through my actions by sharing the love of God with the poor, oppressed, victimized, needy and suffering people of Pakistan."[5] Bhatti was the first—and, to date, the only—Christian to hold a cabinet position in Pakistan.

As a newly appointed federal minister, the stocky and heavily mustachioed Bhatti rolled up his sleeves and hit the ground running. A bachelor who lived a spartan, monk-like existence—at his death, only a Bible, a rosary, and a picture of the Virgin Mary were on his small night table—he worked tirelessly over the next twenty-eight months for the nation's religious minorities. He encouraged interfaith dialogue by establishing workshops and round tables to bring together leaders of the Christian, Hindu, and Muslim communities. He pushed for a five percent quota for religious minorities in the government, proportionate to their percentage in the general population. He agitated for the outlawing of hate speech, for official recognition of non-Muslim religious holidays, and for the protection of property of anyone accused under the blasphemy laws. This last measure was particularly important, since merely being arrested for blasphemy was often viewed by Muslim neighbors as an open invitation to loot the accused's home. Bhatti also set up a twenty-four-hour crisis hotline for victims and their families to report minority-directed violence. As his brother Paul once said, Shahbaz was "a symbol [of religious freedom] not just for Christians but for other minorities, and even for very many Muslims."[6]

Bhatti's work brought him his share of death threats over the years, not to mention harassment from the government. But he insisted that such difficulties, while obviously unwelcome, strengthened both his Christian faith and his commitment to speaking up for religious minorities. In an interview shortly before his murder, Bhatti spoke about his precarious situation and how his commitment to Christ gave him the courage to face it.

I want to make it clear that I am mindful that in the struggle to protect the religious freedom, the rights of minorities, and to raise the voice against the blasphemy law, I can be assassinated. I can be killed. But I will continue to follow the principles that I believe. I will continue to raise the voice of the voiceless. And I will not feel fear because of these threats because I follow Jesus Christ who has given his own life for us. So as a follower of Christ, my destiny is to speak up for those who cannot speak up for themselves. I will consider— this is the important phrase I am trying to say—myself most fortunate if Jesus Christ will accept the sacrifice of my blood to raise the voice for the justice and rights of the persecuted and victimized Christians and other minorities in Pakistan.[7]

Death threats against Bhatti accelerated in the volatile days after he publicly praised Salmann Taseer and condemned his murderers. He became the number one target of Pakistan's militant Islamicists, and their public threats against him grew so hair-raising that Bhatti's eighty-eight-year-old father suffered a fatal heart attack under the pressure of worrying about his son. After the old man's death, Bhatti made a point of visiting his grieving mother each morning before going to his government office. He sensed that his time was limited, and he spoke of his premonition to his friend Alexander John Malik, the Anglican bishop of Lahore. Malik urged Bhatti to leave the country for a few months until the situation calmed down, but he refused. His place, he said, was in Pakistan.

It was during one of his daily visits to his mother that he was murdered. On March 2, 2011, he and his driver had just pulled away from his mother's home when their vehicle was abruptly stopped by three or four masked gunmen. The driver, sensing danger, instinctively ducked under the steering wheel just as the assassins opened fire. Bhatti was hit more than twenty times. After looking through the shattered window to make sure that their target was mortally wounded, the gunmen scattered some pamphlets on the street announcing that Bhatti had been executed in the name of Allah. Pakistan's first Christian cabinet member died before reaching a hospital. The memorial service he had planned for Salmann Taseer was to have been held in three days.

Four months earlier, Bhatti had filmed a statement to be released in the event of his violent death. In it, after acknowledging that Islamicists had targeted him, he insisted that their "threats and warnings cannot change my opinion and my principles." Then, in a striking confession of faith, he said: "I want to share that I believe in Jesus Christ, who has given his own life for us. I know what is the meaning of Cross and I'm following the Cross. And I'm ready to die for a cause."[8]

When news of his murder was broadcast, reactions in Pakistan expressed either deep sorrow or jubilation. One Islamabad Christian interviewed by the BBC seemed stunned with grief. "We have been orphaned today," he said. "Now who will fight for our rights?" Expressions of outrage from the Western democracies and the Holy See quickly followed. A Taliban spokesman, on the other hand, was unapologetic. After labeling Bhatti a "known blasphemer of the Prophet," he promised that any other Pakistani who spoke out against the blasphemy laws would meet the same fate.[9] Pakistan's grand mufti deflected responsibility for the assassination by insisting that Bhatti's murder was a plot on the part of the Western powers to "defame" Islam. When Pakistan's prime minister called for a moment of silence in Parliament to honor Bhatti, seated members of a right-wing Islamicist party protested. In death as in life, Bhatti was scorned by many of his fellow Pakistanis.

After his assassination, the Pakistan government appointed another Christian to replace Bhatti. But his successor's position was downgraded to noncabinet status, most likely to mollify Muslim hardliners, and consequently has little if any voice in decision making. At the same time, largely because of the international community's condemnation of Bhatti's assassination, Pakistan's UN delegation moved a resolution to encourage "a global dialogue for the promotion of a culture of tolerance . . . and diversity of religions and beliefs."[10] The resolution passed, creating some good PR for Pakistan. But it's doubtful that it will make much of a difference within the nation's borders. More than three years after Bhatti's murder, the blasphemy laws remain on the books, and Christians and other religious minorities are still harassed, arrested, and imprisoned. Despite the fact that the Pakistan Taliban immediately claimed credit for Bhatti's death, no arrests have been made. The case is still officially unsolved, and that's precisely where spokespersons for the All Pakistan Minorities Alliance, cofounded by Bhatti, fear it will remain.

Within days of his death, the General Assembly of the Catholic Bishops Conference of Pakistan sent a petition to Rome requesting that Bhatti be officially declared a martyr. Canonizing Shahbaz Bhatti, the bishops stated in their petition, would put a face to all the victims of religious persecution imprisoned, tortured, or killed for their faith in the last century. As patron saint of Christian minorities everywhere, Bhatti would be a sign of courageous hope to those likewise called to live their faith in hostile environments. Thousands of people across the world have joined their voices to the bishops in requesting that Rome honor Bhatti. He doubtlessly would've been bewildered by all the attention. As he once said of himself, all he wanted to do was to "make this world beautiful by delivering a message of peace, togetherness, unity, and tolerance."[11]

Judged from the world's perspective, Shahbaz Bhatti may look like a failure. He dedicated himself to ending Pakistan's persecution of religious minorities. Because the injustice continues to this day, some might say that Bhatti's life's work was for naught and his death a tragic waste.

But it's well to keep in mind what Mother Teresa, founder of the Missionaries of Charity, once said: God doesn't require us to succeed, but only to try. Whether or not he's officially canonized, Bhatti's moral courage in defending the rights of people of different religious traditions to worship God in their own way—a courage ultimately fueled by his radical trust in Jesus Christ—nudged the world a bit closer to the Kingdom of God. To the worldly, the movement is imperceptible. But to those who trust in the eschatological vision of a redeemed world, the fact that Bhatti stayed the course to the end is both a testament and a victory. His mission—his destiny, as he said—was to speak out. And he did.

10

THE NICKEL MINES AMISH

we can't be forgiven if we don't forgive

We live in a culture that values self-assertiveness, standing up for yourself, not taking any guff from anyone. Parents teach their children to face down schoolyard bullies and, if slighted in some way or another, many adults eagerly await—and think they're owed—an opportunity for payback. Vengeance, often dressed up in the rhetoric of justice or fairness, seems the order of the day. Nor are religious people exempt from the urge to strike back, as sadly attested by the acts of "divinely sanctioned" violence that persons of faith too often commit or allow to happen.

Put another way: the virtue of forgiveness isn't high on our list of cultural values. In fact, it's frequently written off as weakness. Even those of us who pay occasional lip service to forgiveness often fail to act as if we really believed our own words. That's why so many people were astounded, and more than a few irritated and even angered, at a remarkable act of forgiveness that took place in late 2006 in an Amish community in rural southeastern Pennsylvania. It requires remarkable moral courage to go against the engrained norm of payback. But the Amish, who more than most Christians prefer loyalty to Christ's teachings to popular culture, displayed it.

Nickel Mines, named after the mining operation located there that tapped out at the end of the nineteenth century, is home to many Amish families. The Amish hail from a branch of sixteenth-century Anabaptism, one of the movements that emerged during the Protestant

Reformation. Anabaptists, so called because they rejected the practice of infant baptism (the name means "baptism over again"), preached nonviolence, refused to take oaths or serve in the military, and strove to live according to the teachings in the Sermon on the Mount. Two Anabaptist branches, the Mennonites and the Amish, began migrating to North America as early as the late seventeenth century, settling heavily in what is now Pennsylvania and, later on, in Ohio and Indiana. Mennonites and Amish both remain loyal to their Anabaptist roots. But Mennonites gradually accommodated to the prevailing culture to a greater degree than the Amish, who to this day live as separate from the contemporary world as they can. They eschew electricity and cars, dress and live distinctively, still speak a German dialect among themselves, and refer to their non-Amish neighbors as "outsiders" or "English." Because of their embrace of nonviolence, they're sometimes called "the gentle people."

A 1972 Supreme Court decision exempted the Amish from sending their children to public schools. Instead, they educate them in Amish-run schools up to the eighth grade, at which point the fourteen-year-old boys are apprenticed to a trade such as woodworking or farming, and the girls are taught household skills. While they're in school, Amish kids learn the three traditional Rs as well as a heavy dose of the fourth one: religion.

It was in one of those simple schools that the 2006 Nickel Mines tragedy took place. It was a single-roomed building with one teacher and twenty-six students, aged six through thirteen, from ten local homes.

On that Monday morning, October 2, the school day began as usual. The teacher, a twenty-two-year-old Amish woman, read a passage from the Bible, led the students in a German recitation of the Lord's Prayer and the singing of a few hymns, and then got down to the business of teaching. At ten o'clock she sent her students outside for morning recess.

Just after the kids were called back in fifteen minutes later, a local milk truck driver named Charles Carl Roberts IV backed his pickup right up to the school's front porch and banged on the door. Holding up a metal object, he asked the teacher if she and her students could help him search for its mate, which he claimed had fallen off the underbelly of his truck. But in just a matter of seconds, the visitor pulled out a semiautomatic pistol. The teacher managed to get away and ran to the nearest house to call 911. After her departure, Roberts told all the boy students to leave but ordered the ten girls to remain. After binding their hands, he fetched a few more weapons from his pickup, brought them into the school, nailed the front door shut, and pulled the blinds. He made it clear to the frightened girls that he intended to rape as many of them as he could. The younger ones didn't understand what he meant. Some of the older girls who did begged him to take them first, hoping to spare the young ones.

By 10:45, state troopers had surrounded the schoolhouse in response to the 911 call. One of them shouted to Roberts through a bullhorn, asking him repeatedly to come out peacefully. But the appeals only seemed to agitate and anger the already distraught gunman. Ten minutes after they began, he rang 911 and told the operator that if the troopers didn't back off he would start killing the girls. "Right now, or they're dead in two seconds," he warned. "Two seconds!" The police pushed their perimeter back a few more yards from the schoolhouse and considered their options. But twenty minutes later, before they had worked out a strategy, they heard three shotgun blasts from the school, followed by the rapid fire of a semiautomatic weapon. They rushed the building and broke through the windows. Roberts fired once at them and then turned his gun on himself.

Inside the gun smoke–filled room, the troopers found the ten girls. Roberts had lined them up and then sprayed dozens of rounds into them. Five died; the other five were all critically wounded. Broken glass, blood, and bits of body tissue were scattered across the floor. The walls were pocked with bullet holes.

An explanation of why the thirty-two-year-old Roberts assaulted the school, took hostages, and then gunned them down came out slowly in the days that followed. Some of the wounded girls remembered that he had said to them, "I'm angry at God and I need to punish some Christian girls to get even with Him."[1] Nine years earlier, Roberts's wife had given birth to a daughter, Elise, who lived less than a half hour. Since then, he had been depressed and enraged at God for letting his daughter die. In a suicide note that he left for his wife and three children, he wrote, "I'm filled with so much hate towards myself, hate towards God, and an unimaginable emptiness. It seems like every time we do something fun I think about how Elise wasn't here to share it with us and I go right back to anger."[2] His plan to rape and murder the Amish school kids was his way of retaliating against a God whom he believed had wronged him. He was going to get even by savaging God's beloved, Amish children. God took his Elise away from him. It was payback time.

The media quickly dubbed the shooting the Nickel Mines School Massacre. Reports of it flooded the airwaves and cyberspace, partly because the victims were school girls, but partly, too, because they were Amish. It was unimaginable, even to a world saturated by and to some extent inured to violence, that anyone would want to hurt the gentle folk or their children. But the initial horror the story evoked was soon accompanied by an equally incredulous amazement when the media reported that before the day was out, local Amish had visited Roberts's widow and children as well as his parents to comfort them for the shame and sorrow they now bore. Moreover, Amish elders, speaking for their community, announced that the gentle people forgave Roberts for what he'd done. Refusing to forgive, said one of them, much less seeking vengeance or retaliation, "is not an option." Forgiving was simply "a normal part of our living."[3] Another pointed out that "we can't be forgiven if we don't forgive."[4]

As the story spread around the globe, financial gifts from literally dozens of countries began to flow into the Nickel Mines Amish community. People wanted to express their sympathy and solidarity with the Amish by helping to pay down the enormous medical expenses for the five girls who were still alive. The inflow of funds was unexpected by the Amish, but they immediately set up an "Accountability Committee" to oversee how the money, eventually more than $4 million, would be spent. Unanimously, the committee members agreed that some of it would be used to look out for the material needs of Roberts's family, left without a breadwinner by his suicide. Amish families also brought cooked meals to the widow and her children. When Roberts was laid to rest the following Sunday in a Methodist cemetery, half of the seventy-five people in attendance were Amish, some of them relatives of the slain and wounded girls.

The public marveled at the generosity with which the Amish forgave Roberts and tended to his family. Many commentators, Christian or otherwise, noted that the world would be a better place if everyone emulated the Amish willingness to forgive rather than following the payback norm. But some dissenting voices, echoing the cultural dismissal of forgiveness as a disguised form of weakness, argued that forgiving under such circumstances was misguided, immoral, or both. Some insisted that only those who have been directly violated have the right to forgive, and that therefore the Amish community had no authority to forgive on behalf of the slain girls. Others argued that forgiving Roberts, however well-intentioned the forgivers might be, amounted to a trivialization of the evil he committed. Such a heinous act, they maintained, demanded retribution. Slaying children—and, moreover, children that the culprit had also intended to rape—is always unforgiveable. Even some of those who accepted that forgiveness is a virtue admitted to ambivalence in this case, again because the victims were children.[5]

These reservations are understandable, but they're also based on a misapprehension of what forgiveness means to the Amish. In the first place, the act of forgiving isn't identical to the act of pardoning. Had Roberts lived, the Amish would've thought it only just that he be punished by the law (short of execution, since they're practitioners of nonviolence) for his crime. Moreover, the Amish don't share Western culture's almost fetishistic regard for individuality. They live in close-knit proximity, extended families often sharing the same house, and think of themselves in communal terms, such that the whole is affected by what happens to the part. From their perspective, it was perfectly appropriate to forgive on behalf of the slain and wounded girls. Roberts hadn't only terrorized and shot their daughters; he had inflicted terrible harm on the entire community.

What the critics of the Nickel Mines Amish also failed to understand was the profound connection the Amish see between forgiveness and living their Christian faith. In neither their public worship nor private devotions do Amish pray extemporaneously. They believe that doing so risks presumptuousness. Instead, they rely on prayers drawn from scripture, and they place special emphasis on the Lord's Prayer, the one that Jesus himself taught his disciples. In it, Jesus instructs us to forgive our debtors, just as we hope that God will forgive our own debts (Mt 6:12). Immediately afterward, Jesus repeats the prayer's recommendation of forgiveness: "If you forgive men their trespasses, your heavenly Father also will forgive you; but if you do not forgive men their trespasses, neither will your Father forgive your trespasses" (Mt 6:14–15). Moreover, the Amish are well aware of Jesus's parable of the forgiven servant who, because he refuses to forgive others, is seized by his angry master and hauled off to jail. "So also my heavenly Father will do to every one of you, if you do not forgive your brother from your heart" (Mt 18:35). Finally, the Amish likewise take seriously Luke's account of Jesus's words from the Cross: "Father forgive them, for they know not what they do" (Luke 23:34).

The scriptural commands to forgive are what undergird the Amish emphasis on forgiveness. To not forgive is to forgo one's own chance of forgiveness. To not forgive is also to risk committing the sin of retaliation, which is always a form of emotional or physical violence. To not forgive is to hold one's own ego in such high regard that any slight to it demands vengeance. To not forgive is to presume that transgressors are always responsible for their actions, when in fact they, like those who crucified Jesus, may know not what they do. To not forgive is a betrayal of both the letter and the spirit of Jesus's teaching.

The Amish have a word that describes the fundamental attitude that lies behind their embrace of forgiveness: *Uffgevva*. It means relinquishing one's will to God's. According to one of the Nickel Mines Amish, "that's what our life is all about. It's the biggest thing about being Amish."[6] *Uffgevva* oughtn't to be interpreted as a kind of fatalism that passively shrugs its shoulders at whatever happens as irreversibly intended by God. Instead, it's a willingness to respond to whatever happens in a way that is pleasing to God. The Amish don't believe that a good and loving God somehow preordained or legislated that an obviously psychotic man would one day barricade himself inside a one-room schoolhouse and butcher their children. But they *do* know how Jesus bids them to respond to acts of aggression: with compassion, with fortitude, with patience, and with forgiveness. Forgoing the urge to exact vengeance in such circumstances, no matter how personally satisfying at some level it might be, is an act of *Uffgevva*. It's no easy task. As a mother of one of the slain girls said, "The bitterness may reenter your mind from time to time, and then you have to think about forgiveness again."[7] But it's the right thing to do, and because of it the Amish are also confident that God will help them live in accordance with the divine will. "God wants us to forgive," one of them explained. "Anything he asks us to do, He will also help us to do. We are to pass on to others the same kind of love we daily receive from God."[8]

One of the best known and most loved stories of *Uffgevva* in the Amish tradition, and one that the Nickel Mines Amish occasionally alluded to when questioned about their response to the tragedy, is the 1569 self-sacrifice of their Anabaptist forebear Dirck Willems.

According to *Martyrs Mirror,* a huge compendium of tales of Christian martyrdom found in most Amish homes, the Dutchman Willems, who was charged with heresy by Roman Catholic authorities, was fleeing over a frozen pond when his pursuer broke through the ice and was in danger of drowning. The worldly thing to do would've been to seize on the pursuer's plight as a bit of good luck and to run away, leaving him to his fate. But Willems knew that he was called to embrace God's will, regardless of the personal cost, and in this instance his duty was clear: return and rescue the drowning man, even though doing so would put him in the hands of his enemies. And that's exactly what happened. He rescued his pursuer, who promptly arrested him and carted him off to prison where Willems was tortured before being burned at the stake. The entry on Willems in *Martyrs Mirror* concludes that he endured his suffering "with great steadfastness" and confirmed the faith "with his death and blood, as an instructive example to all pious Christians."[9] What that surely means is that Willems forgave his tormenters, in conformity with what Jesus expected of him, and that in doing so he displayed remarkable courage, or "great steadfastness." *Uffgevva.*

A few weeks after the shooting, Amish men from around the area met together to demolish the Nickel Mines schoolhouse. The decision to tear it down wasn't based solely on the fact that the structure, if left standing, would forever be haunted by what had happened there. It was also made out of worry that the site would become a macabre tourist attraction, drawing hundreds of ghoulish sightseers who would disrupt the equilibrium of Amish life. So within a month after the shooting, the building was gone and the land on which it had sat smoothed over. Today, crops grow on the site.

Exactly six months after the tragedy, on April 2, 1997, the youngsters of the community moved into a new schoolhouse built by Amish carpenters. Christened "New Hope School," it sits off the main road, a bit more deliberately secluded than its predecessor. To help make the transition back to school less traumatic for the children who survived the shooting, police authorities visited on the first day to assure them that they were safe. Roberts's widow and his parents, with whom the Amish maintained close ties, also visited. Four of the five wounded girls were there. The fifth, maimed for life by the bullets that struck her, requires round-the-clock care at her home.

The response of the Nickel Mines Amish to the disaster that befell their community in 2006 is one of the most inspiring examples in our day of the kind of moral courage Christian commitment encourages and fuels. Sustaining both their lifestyle and their values in the face of a culture that finds the first odd and the second quaint is in itself an act of moral steadfastness. It takes determined courage to stand apart from the crowd in any situation, but particularly so for the Amish, who differ so markedly from their English neighbors. The virtue of forgiveness, so important to the Amish, is particularly viewed with suspicion by the culture that surrounds them. Yet they still find the courage to forgive.

The decision of the Amish to forgive Charles Carl Roberts called for moral courage in a second way as well. Forgiveness is only appropriate in the face of evil. Those critics of the Amish who accused them of trivializing evil by forgiving Roberts miss the point that forgiveness is an explicit acknowledgment, not a denial, of evil. If there was ever a situation in which it is nearly overwhelmingly tempting to jettison *Uffgevva* long enough to seek revenge, it is the murder of children. But the Nickel Mines Amish withstood their own private urges toward angry retaliation just as they withstood the pressure of an outside culture that encourages payback. Both are astounding and admirable acts of Christian courage.

11

LI YING

to repay the Lord's grace

Communist leaders in the People's Republic of China aren't especially concerned about a violent uprising threatening their power. The military and police keep too tight a rein upon the nation's 1.3 billion citizens for that possibility to be anything but remote. What keeps China's rulers awake at night is the fear that the ranks of nonviolent dissenters will quietly but steadily swell until a tipping point is reached that irreversibly undermines state authority. A velvet revolution, in which the power structure simply collapses under its own weight because the majority of citizens refuse to recognize or cooperate with it any longer, is the greatest threat to China's ruling elite.

Faith communities, because their ultimate allegiance is to the God they worship rather than to the state, perpetually threaten the stability of any totalitarian regime. By embracing values and beliefs that run counter to those promoted by the state, they create pockets of resistance that challenge, even if only implicitly, the repressive status quo. As such, they must either be destroyed outright or co-opted by the state.

The People's Republic of China uses both tactics to control Christian faith communities within its borders. Religious belief was condemned as an enemy of the "new order" as early as the 1949 communist revolution, but it was during the Cultural Revolution in the 1960s and 1970s that no-holds-barred persecution became the order of the day. With the 1966 launch of the "Destruction of Four Olds" campaign, which declared war on Old Customs, Old Culture, Old Habits, and Old Ideas, thousands of Christians were publicly mocked and condemned in "people's courts," sentenced to hard labor in prison camps, or murdered outright. Churches, religious schools and hospitals, seminaries, monasteries, and even Christian graveyards were demolished. The goal was to wipe away any trace of Christianity—or, for that matter, Buddhism and Islam. Religion of whatever stripe, as Marx famously said, is an opiate.

Following the intemperate days of the Cultural Revolution, China embarked on a largely cosmetic effort to improve its image—not necessarily its policy—when it came to human rights. Although still a self-proclaimed atheist state, China now officially tolerates Christianity within its borders. But the catch is that Christians must belong to a government-approved church body. For Protestants, worship is legal only within the Three Self Patriotic Movement; Catholics must belong to the Chinese Catholic Patriotic Society. Both organizations are largely controlled by the government, as the "Patriotic" in their names suggests. The Three Self Patriotic Movement's stated "unity" goals of self-governance, self-support, and self-propagation are intended to isolate Chinese Christians from interaction with Western ones. Under the auspices of the Chinese Catholic Patriotic Society, the government reserves the right to ordain priests and consecrate bishops without consulting the Vatican. Christianity in China, in other words, is tolerated if it shills for the government.

It's unclear how many Christians actually live in China. The estimated range of membership in the Three Self Patriotic Movement stretches from 16 to 23 million Protestants. Membership in the Chinese Catholic Patriotic Society probably hovers around 6 million. But all told, it's likely that there are nearly 70 million Protestants and 9 million Catholics in the People's Republic, which means that fewer than half of the nation's Christians are officially registered with the government. Most of them, correctly seeing that the two government-sponsored organizations are tainted, choose to worship in unsanctioned house church communities and secret congregations.

And that, from the perspective of the Communist leaders, is unacceptable, because house churches are precisely those pockets of resistance that can birth velvet revolutions. So for the past several years, China has adopted a no-tolerance policy toward them while still maintaining the charade that Christianity is protected by the state. House churches are condemned as dangerous "cults" or "abnormalities" simply by virtue of their refusal to join the Three Self or Chinese Catholic movements. Persecution aimed at eradicating house churches has dramatically ramped up in the last few years, with hundreds of members arrested, tortured, and imprisoned. According to China Aid, a human rights watchdog group, incidents of government-sponsored repression have increased by nearly 400 percent since 2006.[1] In 2011, the Chinese Central Committee, suspecting that Western Christians encouraged the proliferation of house churches, issued a document for "resisting foreign use of religion to infiltrate institutes of higher education and preventing campus evangelism."[2] In each of its annual reports on religious freedom since 1999, the U.S. Department of State has designated China a "Country of Particular Concern" because of its "severe violations of religious freedom."[3]

It takes moral courage for house church Christians to remain faithful in the face of governmental persecution. Additionally, they often endure public hostility. Because the vast majority of Chinese are either indifferent or actively opposed to religion, Christians are frequently refused housing, jobs, or services, and are often socially harassed or ostracized. So the pressure to join the two state-approved Christian organizations, to keep one's religious convictions private, or to renounce the faith altogether, is constant and severe. Given China's information lockdown, accounts of individual Christians who have resisted the pressure are hard to come by. But we do know about some of them. One is Li Ying, a forty-eight-year-old member of the South China Church, one of the People's Republic's largest outlawed house churches.

South China Church was one of several offshoots from an independent church, alternately known as the All Ranges, Total Scope, or New Birth Movement, founded by Chinese activist Peter Xu in defiance of the Cultural Revolution's persecution of Christians. Headquartered in central China's Hubei Province, South China began sometime in 1990 or 1991. Fundamentalist and charismatic in theology and tone, as most Chinese house church movements are, the church was headed by Gong Shengliang ("Shengliang" means "holy light"). Thanks in large part to his leadership, the church's growth was impressive, with branches quickly springing up in a dozen provinces throughout central and south

China. At its peak, the South China Church may well have had a hundred thousand members.

One of them was Li Ying, Gong Shengliang's niece. Most of what we know about her comes from the "Testimony of Sister Li Ying," a semi-autobiographical sketch published by China Aid.[4] The document, translated into often awkward English, is both a chilling account of the hazards of openly professing Christianity in China and an inspiring portrait of a woman who dared to do so.

Li, born in Hubei Province, was the eldest of five siblings. Her mother was a fourth-generation Christian, and in turn raised her children in the faith. Apparently the marriage of Li's parents, arranged by a matchmaker, was rocky. Although her father later became a rather rigidly thinking Christian who was eventually jailed by the authorities, he appears not to have been sympathetic with the faith during Li's childhood, nor was he much of a provider for his family. Although a good student, Li was forced to quit school at an early age to care for her younger brothers and sisters while her mother worked. According to the "Testimony,"

> The poverty of her family taught her thriftiness since childhood and she treasured every piece of pencil and other school utensils. She would pick up three baskets of firewood for cooking the three meals at home everyday[sic], when her younger brother grew older. During summer vacation she had to cut grasses to feed sheep, cows and pigs, and even traded in her grasses and sometimes helped grown-ups thresh wheat on the threshing ground in the evening to supplement family income and alleviate difficulty.

Li was sustained through the hard times by a strong Christian faith. As a child, she was fond of hymn-singing and prayer. After she learned to read, she devoured the Bible. Itinerant preachers from independent churches frequently visited her neighborhood and sometimes stayed at her family's home. She would listen to them for hours, often moved to tears by their words, and soon begin to feel the stirrings of a vocation. "She admired preachers and dreamed of herself becoming one some day in the future."

By the time she was in her late teens, Li began attending the house church of her uncle, Gong Shengliang. At around this same time, she was either married or engaged to be married; the record isn't clear. But what is clear is that the relationship was terminated because of "her dedication to the evangelical ministry for salvation and blessing." Reading between the lines, Li's husband or fiancé felt he was playing second fiddle to her work for God. The breaking point in their relationship seems to have been a "born again" conversion Li experienced when she was twenty that gave her

> a clear vision of her own salvation under blessing and became even more dedicated to the Lord and strengthened her faith without any doubt. The Lord's life inside her was also urging her and she felt that it was imperative to repay the Lord's grace, to preach the Gospel to those suffering and wandering, and water those hungry and thirsty souls with the Lord's Word. All these motivations and passions in her heart compelled her to cast aside the household chores and the family that needed her care, and embark on the road of evangelism.

Li was soon dispatched to Sichuan Province with the task of establishing new branches of the South China Church. She began teaching "theological classes" there—probably more like what we in the West think of as Bible study circles—and became noted for her devotion; the "Testimony" speaks of the calluses on her knees formed by frequent prayer. Li herself reported that during these years of evangelizing, she enjoyed "the closest relationship with the Lord. . . . Whenever I thought of the Lord sacrificing himself and shedding his blood and myself being chosen by the Lord, my tears would be rushing out without stopping."

Li's time in Sichuan wasn't without difficulties, however. There appears to have been a theological feud among the new converts about whether they should focus exclusively on cultivating a personal relationship with Christ or build up the institutional church. Li saw no incompatibility between the two positions, but reconciling the disputants was a laborious and at times discouraging task. Meanwhile, the authorities, alarmed at the proliferation of nonregistered Christians in Sichuan, decided to do something about the situation. During a 1991 retreat whose purpose was to promote unity among spatting church members, security police surrounded the meeting house and arrested everyone inside. The participants were hit with heavy fines, but Li, as a leader in the Sichuan church, was singled out for special mistreatment. "The police had somebody curse and humiliate Sister Li Ying and beat her if not obeying orders [*sic*]. She was punished to kneel [*sic*] on the bench for the entire night because she could not perform crouching with her arms stretching backwards."

Undaunted by her treatment, Li threw herself into evangelizing activities over the next five years, traveling to regions as far-flung as Manchuria to spread the Gospel. Her primary work was training mission leaders in each of the areas she visited to continue the ministry after she departed. But in 1996, she ran afoul of the authorities once more when she tried to help a fellow Christian evade police capture. Both Li and her colleague were apprehended, and this time she was sentenced to one year of imprisonment at hard labor.

Li had plenty of opportunity to think about the future of Christianity in her country while serving her penitentiary term. By the time of her release she had come to the conclusion that the dozens of independent Protestant house churches throughout China needed to consolidate in order to maximize both their evangelical opportunities and their ability to stand up to government intimidation. After several rounds of talks with the leaders from a number of different house churches failed to lead to the unity she hoped for, Li decided in 1997 to launch an underground magazine, *Huanan Zhuankan* or the *South China Special Edition*, as a vehicle for encouraging interchurch cooperation. Over the next three years she devoted herself to the project with the same zeal she had brought to mission travels. According to the "Testimony,"

> She designed a daily schedule for herself: getting up every morning at 5, reading a chapter of the Bible and praying, drafting an outline of subject and content for today's [*sic*] writing, washing and writing for about one hour and having breakfast. She would get down to writing immediately after breakfast. She seemed to have countless words to write and would keep on writing until 11 or 12 midnight to sleep everyday [*sic*]. Once she wrote more than 40,000 characters on Chinese church history in 20 days. She used up countless pencils and piles of paper for writing her manuscripts. The middle finger of her right hand grew a thick layer of callus, and her right shoulder got hurt due to long time [*sic*] of continuous writing. Parts of the manuscripts that she wrote and compiled were published on [*sic*] issues 1 to 48 of the Journal [*Huanan Zhuankan*], and the unpublished parts piled to a height of 2 to 3 feet. One sister . . . said to her: "Sister Li Ying, I saw that you are thinking of how to write for the Journal all

the time, even the little time when you are out of the bedroom into the bathroom."

The "Testimony's" description of Li Ying's dedication to writing and editing the *South China Special Edition* sounds a bit hagiographic. But given the fervor of her faith and the willingness to spend herself in the service of Christ that she demonstrated during her missionary years, the description probably isn't too exaggerated. That the magazine was widely read is attested to by what happened in 2001, the fourth year of its publication. The Hubei police, on orders from Beijing, shut it down, outlawed the South China Church as a dangerous cult, and began arresting its leaders. Li Ying and her uncle Gong Shengliang, the church's leader, were among those nabbed in the roundup.

After her arrest, Li, and most likely some of the others seized along with her, was tortured. The "Testimony" tells us that she endured "consecutive interrogation for 5 days and 5 nights in a row being prohibited from closing her eyes or moving. She sustained a variety of torture and ill-treatment, including beating with electric shock baton, being submerged under water, 'tiger's bench,' 'shouldering sword on back,' etc." When she and the others were brought to trial, they were charged and convicted of the crime of "using a cult to undermine reinforcement of the law." On the strength of testimony given under torture by several women of the South China Church, Gong Shengliang was also convicted of rape. We simply don't know if the charge of rape is true, but the way in which the testimony against Gong was gathered is consistent with Chinese interrogation methods. True or not, the conviction was intended to paint Gong as a diabolical cult leader who used his personal charisma for criminal purposes.

Astoundingly, Li, Gong, and three others were sentenced to death in their 2001 trial. A stunned international community immediately protested with such vigor that panicked Chinese authorities allowed a judicial appeal. At the new trial, the charge was changed, somewhat bizarrely, to "intentional assault." The defendants were once again found guilty, but their death sentences were replaced by prison sentences of various lengths. Li Ying was given fifteen years at hard labor and immediately shipped off to Wuhan Women's Prison. She was released on Christmas Day 2011, after serving ten years of her sentence. Gong

Shengliang, who has suffered a series of strokes since his incarceration, remains behind bars.

Details about Li Ying's years of captivity are hard to come by. As one of the preconditions for her release, the Chinese authorities made her promise to submit to "community correction," and that means in part remaining silent about her prison experience. But while jailed during her two trials, she evangelized fellow inmates. "She began to preach the Gospel to those non-believers, talking about the creation of God, the degradation of men, and how the degraded men need to have God, and teaching them to sing God's hymns. All the non-believers liked to be near her and listen to her talk about God." She "insisted on worshipping, fasting, praying, and singing," and at one point, when jail officials refused to allow friends and relatives to visit her, went on a hunger strike in protest. Although she is reported to have suffered from occasional bouts of depression during her years in Wuhan, there's no reason to doubt that she engaged in prison ministry there just as she had during her two trials.

We know so little about Li Ying. We can sketch with broad strokes her struggle to proclaim her faith in the face of governmental repression and public discrimination, and we can celebrate the strength of character required to undertake and sustain such a struggle. But the political machine in China is skilled, as any totalitarian regime is, in making its victims invisible. A grainy prison photograph and a longish "Testimony," written in the third person and translated into bad English: this is about all we have.[5] Yet even that's enough to give us a good idea of the courage with which she and millions of other Chinese Christians dare to live their faith in a nation bent on either eradicating Christianity or co-opting it as a creature of the government. Given the resoluteness of that grace-fueled courage, how far off can the velvet revolution be?

12

EMIL KAPAUN

ne illegitimi carborundum esse

Maryland native Robert McGreevy, a blunt-spoken cradle Catholic with a strong sense of right and wrong, hasn't gone to Mass in years. The clergy sex scandals were simply too much for him to stomach. But he remains a devout man who says his prayers every night. He once told an interviewer that his devotions begin with the Lord's Prayer and a Hail Mary, both familiar to Catholics around the world. Then, "I pray to *him*: 'Father Kapaun, thank you so much for giving us the courage to keep going.'"[1]

The priest who McGreevy remembers in his nightly prayers perished in 1951 in a prisoner of war camp. Captured two hundred days earlier when his battalion was overrun by Chinese troops in the Korean War's battle of Unsan, Emil Kapaun had already been awarded a Bronze Star for valor. But his bravery under enemy fire was but a lead-up to the extraordinary courage he displayed after he and scores of others in his battalion were captured. Robert McGreevy was one of the prisoners, and he remains convinced to this day that Kapaun's example and care saved him and many of his comrades from dying in the nightmarish camp to which they were sent.

McGreevy's not alone in this. For years after Kapaun's death, dozens of grateful ex-POWS lobbied both government and church officials on behalf of the heroic priest. Their dedication finally paid off when Kapaun was posthumously awarded the Distinguished Service Cross and the Medal of Honor, making him the most decorated military chaplain in U.S. history. At the same time, Rome declared him a "Servant of God," generally considered a preliminary step to beatification. The medals honor his battlefield bravery, but the designation as a Servant of God is a tribute to his moral courage in the prison camp.

There was little in Kapaun's (pronounced KA-pun) childhood and youth that revealed the man he would become. Born to Czech immigrants in the tiny east-central Kansas village of Pilsen (Kapaun would speak with a slight Slavic inflection his entire life), he was a quiet, studious, and devout boy. Working on his father's farm, he became skilled at fixing things, a talent that proved useful later in Korea. He also displayed ingenuity when it came to handling difficult situations. His mother loved to tell of the time he tried to milk a rambunctious cow that only she could handle. After a few unsuccessful attempts, he went to the house and returned to the milking shed dressed in one of his mother's bonnets and aprons. He had no more trouble with the cow.

Kapaun sensed a vocation to the priesthood from an early age, feeling especially called to missionary work. He was accepted by the Columbans, a missionary order, but his family couldn't afford the seminary tuition. So his local priest agreed to finance the boy's education if he trained for parish work instead. Kapaun was a good student, quickly mastering Latin and Greek, and was ordained in June 1940, shortly after his twenty-fourth birthday.

Because he spoke Czech, he was immediately assigned as an assistant in his home parish, ministering to an ethnic Czech congregation. When the priest who had sponsored his seminary studies retired a few months later, Kapaun replaced him. But parish ministry didn't really suit Kapaun. He felt strange about serving people he'd known all his life, especially ones his own age, worrying that they'd think he was putting on airs. There was also a certain restlessness in him, rising to the surface early on in his yearnings to be a missionary, that kept him from settling comfortably in his home parish. Later in Korea, when asked by a soldier why he had signed up for such a hard life when he could've been safe and snug in a Midwest rectory, Kapaun responded, only half-jokingly, "I mean, my God, Bob! Have you ever had to deal with one of those women's committees of a church Altar Society?"[2] On a more serious note, Kapaun explained in a letter written to his bishop that when he was ordained, he had vowed to "spend" himself for God. "This is why I volunteered for the army and this is why today I would a thousand times rather be working, deprived of all ordinary comforts, being a true 'Father' to all my people, than to be living in a nice, comfortable place but with my conscience telling me that I am an obstacle to many."[3]

While serving his parish in Kansas, Kapaun managed to wrangle an additional appointment as an assistant chaplain at a nearby military base. He served there for the first three years of America's involvement in World War II, repeatedly asking, and just as often refused, permission from his bishop to join the army. He finally wore his bishop down in the summer of 1944, enlisted, and after a short period of training shipped overseas. Sent to Burma and India, he flew over five hundred miles a week ministering to the widely spread units under his care. It wasn't exactly the kind of mission work he'd dreamt about as a youth, but it was close enough.

After being mustered out at war's end, Kapaun spent some time earning a graduate degree at Catholic University. Then it was back to Kansas for another parish assignment. But his months in the military had made him even more unsuited for the domesticated life of a parish priest, and his bishop was wise enough to see that. So he gave his blessing to Kapaun's request to go back to the army, just weeks before the Korean War erupted. Assigned to the Eighth Cavalry Division, Third Battalion, Father Kapaun shipped to Korea in July 1950.

The men of the Third Battalion saw combat as soon as their boots hit the ground, and Father Kapaun, although never carrying a weapon, was in the thick of the fighting from the very first. He regularly held masses at the front, using the hood of his jeep as a makeshift altar. He helped retrieve wounded soldiers, often putting himself in grave danger to do so. One such rescue won him his Bronze Star. He usually carried a canteen holder stuffed with apples or peaches he'd somehow scrounged to hand out to soldiers, and everywhere he went he offered kind words and encouragement. When he wasn't in his jeep traveling from one squad to the next, he could be seen making his rounds on an old bicycle he'd picked up somewhere.

All the soldiers who knew Kapaun in those first months of the war were impressed by his coolness under enemy fire. He seemed collected and calm in even the heaviest engagements—once, the rifle fire was so heavy that his ever-present pipe was shot out of his mouth—and his unflappability in turn inspired the troops. They also respected what they sensed as a deep core of authenticity to the man. He wasn't overly pious or judgmental like so many other chaplains, he didn't preach at them, he willingly shared the rigors of their life, even when it came to tasks such as digging latrine pits, and he never complained. He was as capable as any of them of occasionally letting loose a stream of salty language, although he stopped short of taking the Lord's name in vain. He was, in short, a soldier's priest—not merely another "holy Joe," as one of the soldiers who knew him said—and the men of the Third Battalion, regardless of their religious background, genuinely liked him.

By the end of October, the U.S. Army had pushed the North Korean communists north of the thirty-eighth parallel. The men of the Third Battalion had good reason to believe that the war was nearly over and that they'd be returning home soon. The single biggest fear had been that the Chinese would get in the game. But so far they hadn't, and military intelligence was confident they wouldn't.

Military intelligence was mistaken. On the night of November 2, 1950—All Souls' Day—a twenty-thousand-strong Chinese army attacked the much smaller Eighth Cavalry encamped in Unsan, a rural region not far from the Yalu River that separated China and Korea. The Americans were forced to retreat, with the eight hundred men of the Third Battalion ordered to cover the withdrawal of the First and Second Battalions. Fighting was fierce, often hand to hand, as wave after wave of Chinese soldiers assaulted the line. The American perimeter shrank until it was no longer than fifty yards, the situation so desperate that Kapaun gave the men of the Third, Catholic or not, collective last rites. At last given the word to join the Eighth Cavalry's retreat, what was left of the Third Battalion moved out. But the withdrawal was made under such intense enemy fire that there was no choice but to leave the wounded behind. Kapaun, along with Clarence Anderson, an army doctor, refused to abandon them. The two men were captured shortly afterward, and the priest immediately began negotiating with their captors to spare the wounded. At one point, he actually pushed aside the rifle of a Chinese soldier who was preparing to kill one of the injured GIs.

Kapaun, Anderson, and the other men from Third Battalion who were overrun by the Chinese began a northward march in frigid weather to the POW camp that they realized would be their home until they died or were liberated. Kapaun did his best during the march to help the wounded keep up, supporting those able to walk and helping to carry the stretchers of those who couldn't. But many of the soldiers were so weakened by their wounds that they simply couldn't go on, and the Chinese guards escorting the American column would shoot them where they fell.

Once in the camp, it quickly became obvious that the North Korean and Chinese intended to kill their prisoners by inches. The freezing GIs were issued no clothing to help them survive the harsh winter, and the huts in which they were billeted were so shoddily built that they offered little protection against the snow and wind. Prisoners were fed twice a day, receiving each time a handful of raw and nearly indigestible millet and corn that totaled about three hundred calories. There was no fuel to build fires to cook the millet, nor was any potable water provided. The soldiers were left to quench their thirst by eating snow.

Father Kapaun went into overdrive to sustain his fellow prisoners spiritually and mentally. He was everywhere, offering comfort to the despairing, gently chiding others whose hunger led them to steal from their comrades, cheering the forlorn with a joke and a smile, and constantly exhorting the prisoners to hang onto hope. Whenever he made his rounds, he always offered to say a prayer, but he never insisted. At risk of punishment, nightly he would sneak into barracks other than his own to urge the troops to keep their spirits up—and to pass around his pipe to the tobacco-starved prisoners. One soldier remembered that whenever he happened to meet Kapaun in the camp yard, the priest would mutter to him, *Ne illegitimi carborundum esse:* "Don't let the bastards get you down."[4] Occasionally, even the normally cool Kapaun displayed anger at his captors—at one point, for example, he said to a fellow prisoner that he'd enjoy "kicking the ass" of the Chinese camp commander—but no one ever saw him give way to despair. And he always regretted his outbursts of anger. As a Christian, he sincerely believed that he was called to love rather than hate his enemies, and he worked hard to forgive the Koreans and Chinese who abused him and the other prisoners. He also encouraged his comrades to do the same.

But Kapaun knew that the GIs needed something more than spiritual comfort if they were to survive. So he quickly became one of the camp's most artful thieves, "liberating" whatever he could get his hands on—food, clothing, scraps of blankets, chips of wood—for distribution to the prisoners. He also encouraged them to steal whenever they had a reasonable chance of success, and frequently invoked the intervention of St. Dismas, the good thief crucified alongside Jesus. Stealing from an enemy bent on starving or freezing them to death, Kapaun assured the men, was no sin, especially when the lifted goods were shared instead of hoarded.

Calling on his boyhood talent of working with his hands, Kapaun began scrounging pits of tin which he then pounded into pans to boil water. He was so skilled at locking the different pieces together that the pans barely leaked. Each morning, he would rise before the others, collect bits of wood, and build a tiny fire, carefully shielded from the camp guards, with which he boiled water. Throwing a few beans or grains of millet into the water that he'd saved from his own rations, he'd call out a cheerful "hot coffee!" to the awakening prisoners. It seems a small gesture to us. But for men ground down by months of hunger, cold, and homesickness, the creature comfort of a hot drink and kind greeting in the morning was everything.

Given the camp's miserable conditions, diseases encouraged by malnutrition, exposure, and filth began to sweep through the inmate population. Half-starved prisoners fell victim to scurvy and pellagra. (Their hunger was so great that sometimes they would pick and devour undigested seeds out of one another's excrement.) Nearly all of them endured dysentery at one time or another, a particularly dangerous malady given their level of weakness. Pneumonia, especially in that first terrible winter, was also a big killer. A full one-third of the troops captured alongside Kapaun never made it out of the camp alive.

A good part of Kapaun's time each day was spent nursing those inmates who had taken sick. He boiled water to clean them when they soiled themselves, and he scrubbed as best he could the rags that covered their bodies. Lice and scabies were especially prevalent in the filthy camp, and Kapaun often picked them off of prisoners too ill to groom themselves. He also did his best to prevent the guards from hauling sick GIs from their huts to an abandoned Buddhist temple on a nearby hill that became known as the Death House. Guards insisted it was a hospital for the most desperately ill, but the prisoners knew better. POWs taken there were laid out on the bare earth and left to starve or freeze to death. Of the sixty prisoners carried to the Death House, only five ever returned. In camp, sick POWs at least had a chance. And if they died, they died among comrades, not all alone in a forsaken temple.

On Kapaun's arrival at the camp after the terrible march, the Chinese had angrily ripped off the white cloth cross from his helmet that identified him as an army chaplain and dramatically threw it on a trash pile. Kapaun had thought about retrieving it, but then decided to leave it where it was. "The fact that it is lying on this garbage heap," he explained to one of the prisoners, "causes every man to see it and to remind them of their God."[5] Hard as things might get, Kapaun wanted his comrades to be strengthened by the knowledge that they were not forsaken.

Nor did he let the North Koreans and Chinese break the POWs' spirits. All the prisoners testified that one of the greatest burdens of camp life was the mandatory indoctrination sessions held several times a week. Communist propagandists barraged the GIs with jeremiads against capitalism, the American military, and Washington, and offered extra rations to any of the prisoners who would publicly acknowledge the "error of their ways." The indoctrination sessions were deliberately designed to browbeat men already on the edge from starvation and depression. Father Kapaun refused to let that happen.

From the very beginning, he publicly challenged the propagandists at their meetings. He never raised his voice, but consistently rebutted their propaganda and accused them of deception. Following the meetings, he often led the men in songs like "America the Beautiful," not so much out of patriotism as the desire to overcome hopelessness and affirm decency in the midst of cruelty and death. Sometimes, when Kapaun realized that the men needed an even more forceful example of resistance, he gave it to them. Once, after the prisoners had endured a furious harangue by a guard who threatened to shoot all of them on the spot, Kapaun broke the uneasy silence by exclaiming, "What a dumb son of a bitch!" The men broke into defiant laughter.[6]

The camp authorities, already despising Kapaun because he was a priest, went out of their way to discredit or humiliate him. They harassed him, mocking both his religious convictions as well as his appearance; after a few months of prison life, Kapaun was as skeletally thin, unshaven, and filthy as the other men. Resenting his morale-boosting challenges to them, camp propagandists hammered away at him in the indoctrination sessions. But Kapaun, to the delight of his comrades, gave as good as he got. When one of the Chinese propagandists sarcastically asked, "Where's your God now?" the priest responded that God, like the air, was invisible but present everywhere. When another urged the POWs to ask Mao Tse-tung instead of God for their "daily bread," Kapaun, referring to the starvation rations given the men, retorted that if the starvation rations given the prisoners were examples of the daily bread mentioned in the Lord's Prayer, then God must be a terrible baker indeed. His defiance confounded and infuriated his captors. As one of his fellow prisoners later said, "They were plain afraid of him. They didn't know how to treat someone so fearless of them, who paid no attention to them and carried an aura with him."[7]

In the only sermon of his ever recorded, Father Kapaun had noted that in most lives, "there will come a time when we must make a choice between being loyal to the true faith or giving allegiance to something else opposed" to it. "Oh God," he concluded, "we ask of thee to give us the courage to be ever faithful."[8] Kapaun displayed the courage for which he prayed right up to his own death. Sometime in May 1951— prisoners would later disagree about the exact date—the emaciated priest was carted off to the Death House from which he'd shielded so many others. Suffering from dysentery, pneumonia, and a blood clot in his leg, Kapaun simply had nothing left to give. As he was carried away, he raised his right hand to bless the Chinese guards, and then he asked for their forgiveness. The grief-stricken POWs who watched knew that the priest was asking pardon for those times that he had found it hard to forgive his captors. A lesser man might have lost his faith in a loving God, or succumbed to the poison of hatred for the enemy. But from his first to his last day in camp, Kapaun had urged the prisoners not to hate their enemies or to seek vengeance, but to forgive them. That they managed, under Kapaun's guidance, not to let the "bastards" strip them of human decency was yet another reminder of God's presence in their midst. It was also a tribute to the soft-spoken priest whom Robert McGreevy, sixty years later, thanked every night in his prayers.

13

CLARENCE JORDAN

defying the polio of the soul

Clarence Jordan loved to tell what happened on Christmas Eve in 1965 when he tried to attend services at an all-white Baptist church in Americus, Georgia. He was accompanied by several friends, some of whom were black. A furious church elder confronted them as soon as they walked through the door. He accused Jordan of deliberately disrupting the festive occasion by bringing in blacks. "This is our private church!" he sputtered. "I thought this was God's church," replied Jordan. The elder exploded with rage. "That's beside the point!" he shouted.[1]

But for Jordan, it was *exactly* the point. As a Christian, he was convinced that God loved all human beings equally, and that churches, which after all belonged first and foremost to God, were called to mirror that love. To exclude anyone for any reason, especially for the color of their skin, was a sin. It was an assault on the Beloved Community that Jesus had inaugurated through his life, teachings, and resurrection.

Jordan's conviction wasn't merely an abstract belief. For him, it was a way of life, as Jesus intended it to be. In 1942, Jordan cofounded Koinonia Farm, a Christian intentional community whose members tried to live with the simplicity, peacefulness, and radical discipleship displayed by the very first followers of Jesus. Koinonia was integrated from the very beginning, with whites and blacks working, eating, praying, and living together. At the time Jordan established the community, such an arrangement would've been risky in almost any section of the

United States. But in Sumter County, Georgia, once described as one of the "meanest" in the nation when it came to its treatment of blacks, Koinonia was anathema. It took incredible moral courage for Jordan and his associates to stand against the entrenched racism they encountered there, and Jordan more than once admitted that its fury "scared the hell" out of him.[2] But he trusted in God to inoculate both himself and the other members of Koinonia against the paralysis of fear, what he once called the "polio of the soul."[3] By remaining steadfast, his example helped the residents of Americus, and indeed of all America, to examine their hearts.

Koinonia's founder was born in 1912 in the west Georgia town of Talbotton. His family was relatively well-off and highly respected in the small town. As in most of rural Georgia, there was a sizeable black population in and around Talbotton, mostly employed in sharecropping and domestic help. Segregation in every imaginable respect was the norm. Jim Crow ruled.

Jordan was disturbed from an early age by what he accurately saw as a glaring inconsistency between the Christianity professed by everyone he knew and the way in which they talked about and mistreated blacks. On Sundays, the good people of Talbotton went to church and sang hymns and listened to sermons that extolled love. But for the rest of the week, they acted as if the gospel message of brotherly and sisterly love didn't apply to blacks.

Jordan's growing sense that the South's racism was incompatible with Christianity came to a head when he was twelve years old. That summer, he committed himself to Christ at a tent revival. As is usual in such affairs, religious emotions ran high, and the adolescent Clarence felt himself swept away on a wave of good will and love. For him, the highpoint of the entire experience was when the warden of the local jail beautifully and soulfully sang "Love Lifted Me." But that very night he was awakened by screams coming from the jail, located just a few hundred feet from his parents' house. He knew that the same warden whose singing had enthralled him just a few hours earlier was savagely beating one of his black prisoners. The hypocrisy of it all, as he later said, "nearly tore me to pieces."[4]

During the next four years, Jordan became convinced that God wanted him to devote his life to doing something about the system of apartheid that existed in the South. His family had political aspirations for him. (A brother would become a member of Georgia's Supreme Court, and a nephew, Hamilton Jordan, President Jimmy Carter's chief of staff.) But Jordan decided to study agriculture so that he could gain the expertise to help poor black sharecroppers get more return from their backbreaking labor. He enrolled in the Georgia State College of Agriculture.

Like so many young men of his generation and class, Jordan also signed on as a ROTC cadet at Georgia State. But in his senior year, he underwent a second conversion experience after immersing himself in the Sermon on the Mount. Coming to the realization that bearing arms was contrary to Christ's teaching—*"blessed are the peacemakers"*—Jordan immediately resigned his commission and, upon graduation, enrolled in a Baptist seminary in Kentucky. While there, he fell in love with Greek and New Testament studies and earned a doctorate in both in 1936. He married two months after receiving his graduate degree.

For the next four years, Jordan worked in inner-city churches, taught New Testament at a black seminary, and became active in organizations such as the Fellowship of Reconciliation that advocated racial equality and pacifism. But all the while he longed to return to his adolescent dream of working on the land with black sharecroppers. In 1941, he met another Baptist, Martin England, who shared his vision. Together, the two began searching for farmland. They finally found what they were looking for in a 440 acre spread just outside of Americus. The soil had been overworked nearly to the point of exhaustion, and most of its trees had been chopped down. But the price was right—a good thing, because between them the two men could come up with only $57.13— and with the help of a generous benefactor, the property was purchased. Jordan always considered the unexpected donation something of a miracle.

Jordan and England decided right away to call their settlement Koinonia Farm. *Koinonia* is New Testament Greek for "communion" or "fellowship." The farm took its inspiration from the Sermon on the Mount, a text Jordan held in high regard as the "platform of the God movement," and was modeled after the Book of Acts' description of the first Christian communities. "All the believers were together and had everything in common. They sold property and possessions to give to anyone who had need. Every day they continued to meet together in the temple courts. They broke bread in their homes and ate together with glad and sincere hearts" (Acts 2:44–46). "All the believers were one in heart and mind. No one claimed that any of their possessions was their own, but they shared everything they had" (Acts 4:32).

Jordan, England, and the other folks associated with Koinonia intended their community to be a "demonstration plot for the Kingdom of God." Their hope was to model an alternative to both the segregationist South and to the materialistic North. As they would soon discover, however, their effort to live the Gospel brought angry charges of communism, agitation, and race betrayal.

From the start, Jordan and England envisioned Koinonia as a fully integrated community. White and black seasonal laborers on the farm were paid equal wages, something unheard of at the time in Sumter County. At mealtimes, whites and blacks sat at the same table to break bread together, an act especially offensive to local whites. Later on, several black families became regular workers and residents at the farm, participating as equal partners in community decision making and worship. Christian pacifism, voluntary simplicity, communal ownership, and regular times for prayer and Bible study were the norms. As Jordan wrote years later in a book on Jesus's Sermon on the Mount, he and his fellow Koinonians hoped to live in such a way as to "dethrone race prejudice, militarism, egotism, or any other of the jealous demonic gods who demand respect and obedience from the children of humanity."[5] Koinonia was, indeed, a demonstration plot for the Kingdom of God.

In the community's first years, residents of Americus looked at Koinonia with somewhat bemused tolerance. They were proud to have a PhD-holding Baptist clergyman as a neighbor, and Jordan was often asked to guest preach at local churches. But as the goals of Koinonia became clearer, the cautious welcome extended to Jordan cooled considerably. Jordan's sermons clued his audiences into the fact that the brand of Christianity he was recommending was a long way from the kind they practiced, especially when it came to thinking about race, and their responses ranged from irritation to outrage. At the conclusion of one of his sermons, for example, Jordan watched as an elderly woman, "as crisp with pride as a dead honeysuckle vine," made her way toward him. He could tell from the way she strode and the expression on her face that she was livid. "I want you to know," she told him, "that my grandfather fought in the Civil War, and I will *never* believe a word you say!" Clarence, always gracious but never one to water down the gospel message, replied: "Ma'am, your choice seems quite clear. It is whether you will follow your granddaddy or Jesus Christ."[6]

Local grumbling against Koinonia erupted in its first open clash in 1950. Jordan and several members of the community regularly attended services at the all-white Rehoboth Baptist Church in Americus. One Sunday he brought along a dark-skinned Asian Indian student who was visiting the farm. The ushers were scandalized and tried to block the young man's entrance into the church. When Jordan protested by saying that such inhospitality was unbiblical, one of them shouted—comically, in hindsight—"Don't drag the Bible into this!" Shortly afterward, Rehoboth's elders unanimously voted to exclude any Koinonia Farm worker from membership in the church. War had been declared.

Tension between townspeople and Koinonia simmered over the next few years, especially after school desegregation became the law of the land following the Supreme Court's 1954 Brown v. Broad of Education ruling. Residents of Sumter County seethed at what they took to be the court's interference with their way of life. Eventually, furious at forced integration but powerless to circumvent it, county officials instead lashed out at Koinonia. They issued an injunction against a planned summer camp for black and white kids, citing it as a "moral menace" because children staying at the farm might happen to see cows or pigs copulating. Realizing that the vague citation might not carry much legal weight if challenged, the authorities also insisted that the proposed camp was a "public health menace."

That same year, Jordan agreed to sponsor the enrollment of two black freshmen at an Atlanta business college. This was the final straw for his neighbors. The sponsorship made statewide news, and Americus residents, alarmed that their town was linked by the media to a notorious "nigger-lover," decided that Jordan and Koinonia had to go. The campaign to oust them began modestly enough: threatening phone calls, bullying of Koinonia kids at the local high school, cold shouldering in town. Religious, business, and civic leaders drove out to the farm to meet with Jordan in efforts to convince him that his presence was a disruption of the peace. Surely, they told him, the trouble he and his coworkers were stirring up was offensive to the God he claimed to serve. Jordan replied that he'd been praying a lot on the matter and God hadn't said anything to him about being displeased.

So the pressure was ratcheted up. Town merchants boycotted Koinonia, refusing to buy produce, milk, and eggs or to sell seeds, fertilizers, and farm supplies. Jordan started selling its honey and pecans out of state and impishly marketed the pecans with the slogan, "Help us send the nuts out of Georgia!" In retaliation, angry locals destroyed beehives, chopped down pecan and fruit trees, ruined the engine in Koinonia's truck by pouring sugar into its gas tank, and tore down fences. The farm's insurance was cancelled, and local officials began to harass Jordan about allegedly unpaid back taxes.

And then came potentially lethal violence. The farm's roadside market was dynamited in the summer of 1956; over the Christmas holiday that year, drive-by shooters sprayed the house and farm buildings with gunshot, narrowing missing some of the community's twenty-odd children. The men who lived on the farm began staying awake in shifts to guard the community against more attacks. But despite their vigilance, the rebuilt roadside market was bombed again two weeks after the Christmas shooting.

By January 1957, Jordan had decided that he needed help. So he wrote a letter to President Eisenhower, explaining that his community was under attack and asking for federal protection. Eisenhower's attorney general tersely declined to get involved and the violence continued, directed against both the live-in members of Koinonia and local blacks who worked on the farm as day laborers. The climate grew so threatening that black parents warned their children against even mentioning the word "Koinonia" in public. A couple of months after Jordan wrote Eisenhower, hooded Ku Klux Klan members from around the entire state converged on Americus. They drove to the farm in a convoy of several dozen cars and pickups, loudly denounced its members, and burned a tall cross.

The violence continued all that year. More shots were fired at the main house on the farm. Dorothy Day, the cofounder of the Catholic Worker movement, traveled south from New York City to show solidarity by spending Holy Week with Jordan and his community. She took her turn at a night watch and was actually shot at from a passing vehicle. Sacks of pecans that the farm intended to mail to customers in the North were periodically drenched in turpentine by vandals before they could be sent off. Koinonia members who ventured into Americus unaccompanied got beaten up. And in the summer of 1957, the one locally owned store in town that hadn't joined in the boycott of Koinonia was bombed and destroyed.

Each time one of these assaults occurred, Jordan made sure that the county sheriff was notified and that an official police report was filed. But law enforcement officers and county officials proved just as hostile to Koinonia as private citizens, and no arrests were ever made. In fact, unbelievable as it is, a grand jury accused the farm in 1958 of being a communist front that staged all the attacks on its own property and members to draw media attention and cash in on insurance. The grand jury conveniently ignored the fact that the farm's insurance had been cancelled, in part precisely because of the repeated vandalism inflicted by hostile locals.

Jordan never denied that the firestorm whipped up by his experiment in Christian living frightened him and the other members of the community. At the height of the violence, some of the farm children were actually sent northward out of harm's way. But he was convinced that his fidelity to Christ obliged him to remain where he was, even if it meant a violent end, because doing so was the cost of discipleship. One could be an "admirer" of Jesus, he said, or one could be a disciple. If the first, faith comfortably demanded nothing. But to be a disciple meant a willingness to take up the Cross. "One wonders," he once wrote, "why Christians today get off so easily. Is it because unchristian Americans are that much better than unchristian Romans, or is our light so dim that the tormentor can't see it? What are the things we do that are worth persecuting?"[7] His worry was that the answer to this last question was "Nothing."

What inhibited the kind of discipleship that stirred up persecution was fear, the polio of the soul that, said Jordan, "prevents our walking by faith." There were, he believed, two taproots of fear and the racial prejudice it bred in the South: possessions and custom. Ownership encourages a fear of losing one's possessions and the adversarial attitude that comes with protecting them. Custom lends such authority to perspectives and policies that their holders, terrified at the possibility of them being called into question, fiercely defend them against the slightest challenge. ("My grandfather fought in the Civil War and I'll *never* believe what you say!") It only stands to reason that people who cling to possessions and custom fear anyone who rejects both. "To people whose loyalty is to the world," Jordan noted, "citizens of the kingdom of heaven are subversive agents, dangerous enemies who must not be tolerated."[8]

But the great message of Jesus, he continued, is that we need not be held captive by our fears. Neither our property nor our lives are ours. They belong instead to God. Recognition of this destroys the need to cling and to condemn anything perceived as a threat to ownership of material things, tradition, and beliefs. The liberation offered by Christ belongs to everyone, regardless of skin color or social status. In Christ's eyes, no one is any more privileged than anyone else, because he loves all equally. So what is necessary, above all, is to seek the mind of Christ and act not from the compulsion born of fear, but the freedom born from love. In book after book, from vernacular translations of large portions of the New Testament to studies of the Sermon on the Mount, a scriptural text that he considered to be the heart of Jesus's message, Jordan tirelessly sought to help his fellow Christians break free from fear and tumble into love.

Today, Koinonia Farm is a flourishing Christian intentional community accepted by the citizens of Americus. But by 1968, after nearly two decades of persecution, the farm had fallen on hard times. All but two families had left, and Jordan knew that if the community was to survive it needed to find a new way of expressing its mission. The breath of fresh life needed came that year with the arrival of Millard Fuller and his family. Together with Fuller, Jordan directed his attention to providing low-cost housing to the many black families in Sumter County who lived in direst poverty. He set aside over forty acres on the northern edge of Koinonia to build houses. The first one went up shortly before Jordan unexpectedly died of a heart attack in 1969. It was the start of what would become Habitat for Humanity, an international organization still going strong and led by Millard Fuller after Jordan's passing.

On that sad day of Jordan's death, the Sumter County coroner refused to come to the farm to fetch his body, so Fuller took it to the town hospital in the back of a station wagon. After the autopsy, Jordan's friends placed him in a simple wooden crate and buried him on the farm in a spot where community members often gathered for picnics and Bible study. As his coffin was being lowered into the grave, Fuller's two-year-old daughter, not quite knowing what was appropriate but sensing that something needed to be said, suddenly started singing the

Happy Birthday song. "Happy Birthday, dear Clarence, Happy Birthday to you!"

Clarence Jordan would've loved it.

Part III

Spiritual Courage

14

DIANNA ORTIZ

five loaves and two fishes

In the second half of the twentieth century, Central America was a troubled region. Decades of American imperialism had brought a tiny percentage of its people incredible wealth and power while keeping the rest of the population, mainly peasant farmers, in poverty so extreme that it was virtual slavery. Popular resistance to the oppression in four Central American countries—Nicaragua, El Salvador, Honduras, and Guatemala—eventually led to civil wars whose savagery was horrifying.

Guatemala's was the worst both in terms of duration and death. It began in 1960 and continued for the next thirty-five years. Leftist guerrillas battled government military forces, and in the process an estimated 700,000 people perished. Over 100,000 of them simply "disappeared": kidnapped, executed, and buried, often in mass graves, by death squads. It made little difference whether the Guatemalan government was controlled by military juntas or civilian presidents. The army, bolstered by millions of U.S. dollars, tons of weapons, and intelligence from the CIA, was in control. Over 1,500 Guatemalan officers, many of whom went on to lead death squads, were trained in counterinsurgency tactics and enhanced interrogation techniques at Fort Benning's infamous School of the Americas.

To their credit, the Roman Catholic bishops of Guatemala condemned the government-sponsored terrorism and championed the rights of the poor. In 1988, they issued a pastoral letter calling for land reform, one of the primary goals of the guerrillas and fiercely resisted

by the two percent of Guatemalans who owned two-thirds of the nation's land. In retaliation, the Guatemalan army designated the country's Catholics—the vast majority of its population—"allies of the guerrillas and therefore part of the internal enemy, subject to persecution,
death, or expulsion."[1]

The blowback from the bishops' letter changed the course of Sister
Dianna Ortiz's life, hurling her into a nightmare world of torture and
trauma that nearly destroyed her faith in God and left her permanently
wounded. But she eventually discovered, as St. Paul said two thousand
years ago, that sometimes strength is made perfect in weakness.

Born in 1961 in New Mexico, Ortiz grew up in a large Catholic
family, the middle of eight children. At the age of six, she announced
that she wanted to be a nun. True to her word, she joined the Ursulines,
a religious order whose ministry focused on education and care for the
sick, when she was seventeen. By the time she graduated from college,
she felt called to missionary work in Latin America. Although a Chica-
na, she knew only a smattering of Spanish, but she worked hard at
learning it in preparation for her future ministry. In the meantime, for
the next decade, she taught kindergarten at an Ursuline school in Kentucky.

Sister Dianna was sent to the highlands of Guatemala in 1987 to
teach Mayan children; Mayans make up sixty-five percent of Guatemala's population. The town in which she taught, San Miguel Acatan, had
suffered horribly from both government forces and guerrillas. Everyone
in the town, Ortiz learned, had a relative or acquaintance who had been
disappeared or murdered. At one point, she was told, the military
"came in and said to several women, 'Make tortillas for us. If you don't,
you'll be killed.' So the women made tortillas for the army. Then the
guerrillas came in and cut the women's heads off" in retaliation. No
fewer than seven civilian massacres had taken place in San Miguel
Acatan by the time Ortiz arrived there. "I wanted to do anything I
could," she recalled, "to help the people rebuild their lives."[2] She carefully avoided political discussions, focusing instead on the village children to whom she taught in both Spanish and their native Kanjobal
language. One of the three nuns with whom she lived later said that she
was "like a Pied Piper," with "the kids always around" her.[3]

Almost exactly a year after she arrived in Guatemala, Sister Dianna's
bishop received an anonymous letter accusing her of working with the

guerrillas. Soon afterward, Dianna herself received a similar one. On a visit to Guatemala City, she was grabbed by a man on the street who ominously warned her to leave the country. "We know who you are," he hissed.

It's not clear why Ortiz was targeted. Perhaps it was because she was the youngest American nun in Guatemala, as well as the most recent to arrive in the Mayan highlands. Perhaps it was payback for growing public sentiment back in the States for Presidents Reagan's and Bush's financial and military support of the repressive Guatemalan government. Regardless of the reason, Ortiz's superiors took the threats seriously and acted quickly to get her on a plane out of the country and back to Kentucky. But she didn't stay there long. She felt called to serve Mayan children and insisted on returning to Guatemala.

In October 1989, after Ortiz had been back for a few months, the threats became reality. She had traveled with another Ursuline sister to the city of Antigua for a retreat. While she was praying in the garden of the convent where the retreat was being held, two men, one of them brandishing a gun, approached her. Warning her they would start shooting the other guests if she didn't go with them, they shoved her in the back of a car, blindfolded her, and took her, as she later discovered, to the Politécnica, a military installation located, ironically, not far from the U.S. embassy. And so commenced the twenty-four-hour nightmare that radically changed Ortiz's future and wiped out much of her past.

Sometimes torture is used as an interrogation method. But it takes little insight into the human psyche to recognize that most information gathered by inflicting severe physical and emotional pain upon a subject is notoriously unreliable. People under duress eventually say anything to make the pain stop. More often, then, torture is a means by which repressive regimes intimidate and subdue their citizenry. Torturing captives and then returning them to the general public so that their horrible ordeal becomes widely known is a favorite tactic for inhibiting dissent.

Although she didn't know it at the time, this was the reason Sister Dianna was picked up. She was intended to be, she later realized, "a message board upon which those in power [in Guatemala] would write a warning to the Church to cease its opposition or be prepared to face the full force of the state."[4] The first indication that she had been picked up to be made an object lesson to others was what her captors called the "interrogation game." The blindfolded Ortiz heard them lighting up cigarettes, after which they told her that every time she answered a question to their liking, she would go unharmed, but every time she answered in a way they didn't like, she'd be burned with one of their cigarettes. Yet no matter how Ortiz responded to their questions, her interrogators burned her. When she was examined by a physician after her ordeal, she had over a hundred cigarette burns on her back alone.

After the interrogation game, Sister Dianna thought things couldn't get worse. She was wrong. Still blindfolded, she heard her captors tossing coins to determine who would be the first to rape her. The winner ripped off her clothes. "You'll enjoy this, my little virgin," he said as he held her down and savagely mounted her. When he was finished, he whispered in her ear, "Your God is dead."[5]

At some point during the gang rape that followed, Ortiz passed out. When she came to, her captors lowered her into a charnel pit filled with corpses and dying people, all of them covered with blood from knife and bullet wounds. Finally lifted out, she was then taken to a dark room. The sound of groaning and sobbing soon revealed to her that she shared it with another woman who also had been tortured. Her captors entered the room with a video camera. One of them put a knife into her hand, gripped her fingers in his, and forced her to stab the anonymous woman. "Now," he told her, "you are just like us." It was a crude but diabolical act, making Ortiz both torture victim and torturer.

A few hours later, as her captors prepared to rape her again, she heard one of them call out to someone named Alejandro, who had just entered the room, to come and join in. But seeing what was about to take place, Alejandro cursed the men, first in English and then in what Ortiz recognized as American-accented Spanish. The man told Ortiz that he would take her to the American embassy, that her arrest had been a mistake, but that "we" had tried to warn her. When the car that was transporting her to the embassy got stuck in traffic, she bolted out the door and fled. She eventually made her way to the residence of the Papal Nuncio in Guatemala City, and within forty-eight hours was back in the States.

Prior to her torture, Ortiz, by her own admission, had been religiously and emotionally naïve. God was in his heaven, she had presumed, all was right with the world, and nothing really bad could happen to anyone who put his or her trust in God. Her experience at the Politécnica shattered that childlike innocence. When the first rapist whispered that her God was dead, she didn't have the strength or will to protest. Either God truly was dead or for some unfathomable reason had chosen to ignore her cries for help. In either case, the faith that had sustained her during her first three decades shattered. Sister Dianna continued to plead to God throughout her entire nightmare, but somewhere along the way she ceased actually believing in a deity who would permit such horrors.

The victim of torture never sheds the memory of what he or she endured. Sometimes, the experience is so traumatic that it takes center place in the psyche, shoving everything else to the periphery. This is precisely what happened to Sister Dianna. She was able to recall every detail of her ordeal, but lost all but a haphazard handful of memories of her first thirty-one years. Even large parts of the English language disappeared for her. She had to rely on relatives, friends, and fellow sisters for information about who she had been before she was snatched from the convent garden. Similarly, she spent hours reading a dictionary to relearn words.

For the torture victim, the creak of a door or the sight of a uniformed man can be enough to cause the original trauma to flood back. Sister Dianna's reminder was her pregnancy, caused by the multiple rapes she endured while in captivity. In an effort to escape the memento growing inside her, she opted for abortion, which added to her personal torment rather than diminishing it. She already felt unclean because of the gang rape and guilty because of her "complicity" in the stabbing death of the woman in the dark room. The abortion deepened her sense of unworthiness to be a nun and, indeed, a child of God. To an outsider, this seems a paradoxical position, since Ortiz, who had ceased to believe in God, had literally bound and gagged her Bible, refused communion, and rejected the crucifix as a hopeless symbol of torture. But to a victim of trauma, normal canons of consistency no longer apply. As Sister Dianna wrote in her journal, "God, I don't know who to turn to. I don't even believe in you but yet I talk to you. I feel so raw that I want to die. The memories of the torture are so vivid and are gnawing at me. I don't want to remember the details of this nightmare. Please, God, take away these memories. Please."[6]

Memories of her torture and subsequent self-hating guilt combined to lead Sister Dianna to the brink of sanity and even life itself. She suffered from nightmares and flashbacks, and found it difficult to eat, sleep, or relate to others. "Torture," she discovered, "is calculated to destroy trust and the ability to communicate."[7] She obsessively scrubbed her body with bleach, trying to wash away her "impurities," and she kept a razor blade hidden in her shoe, in case the demons became too much for her to bear. (At one point they did, and she tried to kill herself.) To add to the despair of losing God and her own identity, her Ursuline sisters didn't quite know how to respond to her. As one of them said to her long afterward, "It was like you were a different Dianna, and I didn't have a chance to grieve the loss of the old one, and I was at a loss as to how to relate to the new one."[8] Not that Ortiz wanted anyone to get close enough anyway. "I feel like I contaminate people," she wrote.[9] And even if she wasn't toxic, she no longer felt human. "I am a body without feelings, a shell the animal has abandoned."[10]

As if all of this wasn't enough, the U.S. and Guatemalan authorities, when confronted by the Church about Ortiz's abduction, refused to acknowledge that the mysterious Alejandro was an American agent, as Sister Dianna was convinced, and even insinuated that she had made up the entire story—or, if she hadn't, that she had neurotically exaggerated the severity of her treatment. (After all, one authority said, she had been in captivity for "only" twenty-four hours.) Despite her pregnancy, some also ludicrously suggested that the story was concocted to draw attention away from scandalous lesbianism in the Guatemala Ursulines or, alternatively, that it was a leftist ruse to sour public opinion against President Bush's support of the Guatemalan government.

A few weeks after her return to the United States, Sister Dianna was sent to Su Casa Catholic Worker House, a Chicago residential treatment center for victims of torture. Her stay there was a grueling experience, but it began a healing process of sorts—as Ortiz frankly says, she's still not and never will be whole—that allowed her first to acknowledge her own feelings of rage at her torturers and the authorities in Latin and North America who denied the torture, and second to begin to relate to other people who, like her, had been tortured to the point of becoming "bodies without feelings." Contact with fellow victims both awakened pity in her and allowed her to see that she wasn't totally alone, that she had a community of people who, like herself, had been horribly wounded. They understood, from bitter firsthand experience, what she was going through.

Slowly, painfully, the spiritual despair into which Ortiz had been plunged by her brutal treatment began to ease. She discovered two things. The first was that going through the motions of believing helped her regain her faith in the existence of a good God. She saw that many of the other residents at Su Casa, just as traumatized as she, nonetheless clung to their faith, and in joining them in their prayers she began to feel herself drawn back to God. "Looking around I saw people who had suffered every bit as much as I had, if not more, people who also questioned God's existence, and they were praising and thanking God and asking God's blessing on those less fortunate. Just in case. I went along with it. I sang. Because I wanted to believe." [11]

She also began to read more intensely than she ever had everything about Jesus's life and ministry that she could get her hands on. What started out as an almost desperate effort to reconnect with the comforting Sunday School Jesus she had lost led her to a new and more insightful appreciation of Jesus as a fellow sufferer. Like Ortiz, he also had been tortured and had fallen into despair. "My God, my God, why have you forsaken me?!" In his estrangement, his misery, and his terror, he, like her, surely was initially too self-absorbed to worry about the suffering of others. "For a moment he forgot about the other two men who were being crucified. He forgot about the hungry, the poor, and the oppressed." But still he remained the Messiah. This insight began to liberate Sister Dianna from the crushing weight of guilt she felt over both the abortion and the death of the woman in the dark room. "Scripture was allowing me to see that human weakness doesn't make one wholly evil. God can exist in the midst of it." [12]

As she began to heal—and as an essential component of the process of healing—Ortiz demonstrated her commitment to the worldwide community of torture victims by prodding the U.S. government to acknowledge its complicity in Guatemalan atrocities. Time and again her demands were met with official denials: there was no Alejandro, no U.S.-sponsorship of the Guatemalan military, no collaboration between the CIA and Guatemalan death squads.

When Bill Clinton's administration replaced George H. W. Bush's, the denials continued. It seemed to make no difference which political party occupied the White House. Even after Ortiz observed a public five-week silent vigil and bread-and-water fast, the administration reluctantly released only a few innocuous documents. But the breakthrough finally came in 1996, when the government admitted that it trained Guatemalan officers in the techniques of enhanced interrogation—torture—at the School of the Americas. It was, at long last, a crack in the wall of silence. Ortiz went on two years later to found and for a time head the Torture Abolition and Survivors Support Coalition International (TASSC), an advocacy group for survivors of torture staffed by survivors of torture. She remains a member of its board of directors.

Ortiz's discovery of the vast community of sufferers, and her realization that God exists even in the midst of human weakness and misery, were her routes out of spiritual despair. Her faith today is less rosy than it was in the pre-Guatemala days. But it's more deeply hopeful, founded as it is not on a naïve optimism or a childish demand for a flashy miracle that makes everything all right, but on a profound awareness of the fragility of existence and the suffering that God endures alongside our own. This kind of faith is built on the courage that only grace can fuel.

She still, Sister Dianna says, looks to the Bible for answers, and in the story of the loaves and fishes she found one that has become the centerpiece of her new relationship with God. How, she wondered, could Phillip so readily have obeyed Jesus's instructions to feed the crowd with just five loaves and two fishes? "Phillip is a man who can do the math," and he surely knew that the meager offering would never be enough to do the job. Never.

What Ortiz's courageous battle to come back from despair taught her is what Phillip learned: "math is not enough. You have to take into account the unexpected." You have to realize that life is absurd and unpredictable, and that leaves room for radical hope. Jesus also knew this. He accepted what there was—in this case, five loaves and two fishes—and "didn't complain or despair. He gave thanks to God for them, however insufficient they seemed, and he started passing them out."[13]

In climbing her way out of the pit of despair, so like that dark one filled with corpses into which her captors had thrown her, Ortiz arrived at a new kind of trust. "Take what you have, in an attitude of thankfulness, and give what you have, in an attitude of faith, and it will be enough. It will be more than enough."[14] This, she thinks, is what God had been trying to tell her all along.

15

WALTER CISZEK

learning to see as God sees

He wasn't the sort of kid who seemed a likely candidate for the priesthood. Even his father said so. But once Walter Ciszek made his mind up, nothing swayed him. "I was born stubborn," he said of himself.

Raised in a Pennsylvania mining town whose residents were largely ethnic Poles, Ciszek was a stocky boy who soon learned to assert himself with fists and swagger. "I was a bully, the leader of a gang, a street fighter—and most of the fights I picked on purpose, just for devilment."[1] He was always getting into trouble. At one point, his exasperated father marched him down to the police station and demanded—unsuccessfully—that his son be sent to reform school. It came as a colossal surprise to everyone, including Walter, when he announced at the age of thirteen that he was going to be a priest. His father's reservations about his vocation only fed the boy's stubborn determination, and in just a few months he'd left the mountains of Pennsylvania for a seminary near Chicago.

Although training for the priesthood, Ciszek still thought of himself as a tough guy, and to prove it he refused to adopt the often saccharine piety of his fellow students. He also secretly embraced a severe regimen of discipline and self-denial. He sneaked down to the chapel at night when everyone else was asleep to keep long prayerful vigils. He got up early to jog along nearby paths or to swim in the frigid seminary lake. He periodically restricted his diet, sometimes eating nothing but bread and water for days on end. He gave up baseball, even though he loved the game. He felt compelled to test his mettle by doing things the hard way.

While in seminary, Ciszek stumbled across a biography of Stanislaus Kostka, the sixteenth-century Polish saint who defied both familial and social expectations to join the Jesuits. Ciszek liked Kostka's streak of stubbornness, and he gradually decided that he wanted to be a Jesuit too. One of his attractions to the order was its insistence on a strict, military-like obedience. Ciszek had never been good at following rules. But as a tough guy, he could think of no better challenge than voluntarily embracing Jesuit discipline.

He wrote a letter to the Polish Jesuits, hoping to enter the order in Warsaw, but they advised him to stay closer to home by consulting with the Jesuit Provincial at Fordham University, in the Bronx. Ciszek immediately hopped a train to New York City, found his way to the Provincial's office, and demanded to see him. Told that the Provincial wasn't in, Ciszek parked himself outside his door until he returned late that night; Ciszek refused to leave until he was accepted as a Jesuit novice. That was in 1928.

Ciszek got off to a rocky start. His insistence on being a tough guy who was disdainful of his fellow novices, most of whom were a few years younger, almost immediately got him into trouble with his superiors. But he soon tempered his behavior and attitude and got through the next few years of Jesuit training without a hitch. In 1934, his superiors sent him to Rome's Collegio Russico, or Russicum, to study the Oriental Mass in preparation for covert mission work inside the Soviet Union. The moment Ciszek had heard of the plan to slip Catholic priests posing as members of labor gangs into Russia, he knew that this was what he wanted to do. What greater challenge could there be than mission work in an officially atheistic nation? Already fluent in Polish, he labored hard at learning Russian.

By the time Ciszek was ordained in 1937, he was ready and eager to go into Russia. But by then, the Vatican had begun to have second thoughts about the slightly cloak-and-dagger scheme and put it on hold. A disappointed Ciszek was assigned to a Jesuit mission in Albertyn, Poland. Less than a year later, the mission was closed when World War II began and the Soviets occupied eastern Poland. Taking advantage of the chaos of war and the Soviet Union's desperate need of workers, Ciszek and two other Jesuits, passing themselves off as Poles, traveled to the Ural Mountains deep within Russia to work in a lumber camp. Their hope was to minister secretly to their fellow workers, but things didn't work out. They failed to find a receptive audience in the camp. In June 1941, on the very day that Germany invaded the Soviet Union, the three Jesuits were arrested and charged, rather incongruously, with being spies for both Germany and the Vatican. Apparently, the NKVD, the Soviet security police, had been watching them for some time.

After spending a few weeks in a filthy and cramped cell, the three men were split up, and Ciszek soon found himself transported to Moscow's dreaded Lubyanka prison. Built in the late nineteenth century to serve as the All-Russia Insurance Company's lavish headquarters, Lubyanka was a huge yellow brick building with marble columns and parquet floors. Taken over by the Soviet secret police after the October Revolution, it became the place of choice to interrogate—and often summarily execute—political prisoners and "enemies of the state."

Unlike his previous squalid and noisy jail, Ciszek's Lubyanka cell would've reminded him of a hotel room were it not for the iron bars and sheet of tin covering the window. It was neat and clean, with white-washed walls and a relatively comfortable bed. Except for the daily trip under guard to empty his slop bucket, the delivery of his meager breakfast, lunch, and supper, and periodic interrogation sessions with NKVD officials, Ciszek was totally isolated from other humans. He would remain in solitary and for the most part silent confinement in Lubyanka for five long years.

In *With God in Russia*, a best-selling memoir about his Soviet ordeal that he published in 1966, Ciszek's description of his years in Lubyanka is pretty benign. He admits that he was always hungry and that the interrogations were unpleasant. But he focuses primarily on a description of his daily routine that included physical exercise, scheduled prayer and meditation, and a lot of reading from books in the prison library. He plowed his way through so much Russian and German literature that he referred to his imprisonment, almost affectionately, as "Lubyanka University."[2]

But the truth is that Ciszek sugarcoated the brutality of his years in Lubyanka. It's not entirely clear why. Certainly he wanted his book to inspire readers, and he might've feared that telling the whole truth about his ordeal was more than they could handle. It's also the case that he wrote during a time when American priests were generally seen by the faithful as somehow above normal human weaknesses and failings. So Ciszek may have felt inhibited about telling laypeople what really happened to him in Lubyanka because it would've meant revealing the man behind the collar.

Seven years later, he had a change of heart. In a follow-up memoir, *He Leadeth Me,* Ciszek admitted that he hadn't told the whole truth in his earlier book and that he wished to set the record straight. His second book is much better than his first, precisely because in revealing his own spiritual agony in Lubyanka and the remarkable courage with which he faced it, he gives the rest of us guidance in how to survive and learn from our own spiritual crises.

Immediately upon his seizure by NKVD agents in the Urals, Ciszek admitted to a "sinking feeling of helplessness and powerlessness" as the realization sank in that he was "completely cut off from everything and everyone who might conceivably help." His sense of abject impotence only deepened when he was transferred to the "total and all-pervading silence" of Lubyanka.[3] None of his Jesuit superiors, much less his family and friends, knew where he was, or even if he was still alive. His dreams of serving God in Russia were shattered. He felt useless as well as powerless.

The incessant interrogations added to Ciszek's misery. A single session might last for a couple of sleepless days and nights, with two partnered NKVD inquisitors, sometimes playing good cop and bad cop, relentlessly goading him to "confess" his crimes. When his interrogators grew impatient with his refusal to tell them what they wanted to hear, he was punched, thrown to the floor, and threatened with death.

The solitude, the heavy silence, and the emotional and physical exhaustion began to take their toll, and the tough guy identity that Ciszek had cultivated his entire life started to crumble. "Under the gentle prodding of grace," he slowly realized that the strong will he'd always considered to be his greatest strength was in fact a weakness.[4] His decision to become a priest, to join the Jesuits, to go to the Soviet Union: he'd told himself he was doing them all for the greater glory of God. But in fact, they were largely acts of self-assertion. It was *his* will, *his* desires, which had come first. In his arrogance, he'd just assumed that whatever he wanted, God wanted as well. His self-love had drawn him away from God and ever deeper into a foolishly destructive self-reliance that had landed him inside Lubyanka Prison.

It was at this moment of shattering self-awareness, Ciszek recalled, that "the blackness closed in around me completely." He fell into despair. "I had lost not only hope but the last shreds of my faith in God. I had stood alone in a void . . . I had lost the sight of God."[5]

In spiritual terms, Ciszek was enduring a purgative stripping away of everything that he thought he knew about himself and what God wanted from him. It was an agonizing process, because every familiar landmark that once oriented him through life suddenly became alien. He felt the forlornness of a stranger in a strange land. Many people, when they hit this dreadful bottom, never climb out of it. Their despair becomes a permanent part of who they are. Hope dies, and with it joy and sometimes decency. Despair is the worst of sins because it is a refusal to trust, and thus a rejection of God.

Ciszek didn't succumb to the black hopelessness that threatened to swallow and dissolve him. Instead, sensing the danger he was in, he did exactly the thing anyone in such circumstances should do, even though it's counterintuitive: he threw himself headlong into the darkness, trusting as best he could that he would land in the arms of God. It was a great risk, hurtling himself into the abyss. But he knew that doing nothing was soul destroying.

> I knew I had to seek immediately the God I had forgotten. I had to ask that that moment of despair had not made me unworthy of his help. I had to pray that he would never again let me fail to remember him and trust in him. I pleaded my helplessness to face the future without him. I told him that my own abilities were now bankrupt and he was my only help.[6]

As he faced the darkness and prayed to the God he hoped was in it, Ciszek recalled Jesus's words at Gethsemane. "Not my will, but yours," Jesus had said, and in remembering this great cry of humility and obedience, Ciszek suddenly recovered his balance.

> If my moment of despair had been a moment of total blackness, then this was an experience of blinding light. I knew immediately what I must do, what I would do, and somehow I knew that I could do it. I knew that I must abandon myself entirely to the will of the Father, and live from now on in this spirit of self-abandonment to God. And I did it. I can only describe the experience as a sense of "letting go,"

giving over totally my last effort or even any will to guide the reins of my own life.[7]

Ciszek was a man who had always displayed a great deal of determination in his life, even if at times it bordered on bravado. But he graduated from self-will to spiritual courage when he allowed his darkest despair to lead him to the God who awaited him at its center and to give himself completely over to God. In the Lord's Prayer, Christians regularly pray, "God's will be done," and all of us at one time or another have echoed Jesus's "Not my will, but yours." But human frailty being what it is, we find it difficult to subordinate our will to God's and easily fall into the trap of expecting God, as Ciszek wrote, "to accept *our* understanding of what his will ought to be and to help us fulfill *that*, instead of learning to see and accept his will in the real situations in which he places us daily."[8] It takes an incredible amount of courage to abandon self-direction, to let go, as Ciszek did, the reins of one's life.

The insight that came to Ciszek during his dark night was that subordinating his will to God's was the secret of genuine freedom. He had always assumed that freedom was identical to self-sufficiency. Now he saw that freedom consisted in liberation from the destructive delusion of total self-reliance. True freedom is the trust, vitalized by grace, that the concrete situations we find ourselves in, no matter how humdrum on the one hand or perilous on the other, are opportunities to do God's will. They may not be the situations we would've chosen ourselves; most likely, they won't be. But the spiritually free person sees them as part of God's plan.

> The plain and simple truth is that [God's] will is what he actually wills to send us each day, in the way of circumstances, places, people, and problems. The trick is to learn to see that—not just in theory, or not just occasionally in a flash of insight granted by God's grace, but every day. Each of us has no need to wonder about what God's will must be for us; his will for us is clearly revealed in every situation of every day, if only we could learn to view all things as he sees them and sends them to us.[9]

It's important here to be clear on what Ciszek isn't saying. Misread, his words might suggest a kind of fatalism that passively accepts whatever happens, no matter how destructive or hurtful it may be, as aspects

of a prearranged divine plan. But this shrugging-of-the-shoulders attitude in the face of suffering and evil is the opposite of what Ciszek has
in mind. Knowing that God's will for us is to be in the situation in which
we find ourselves doesn't necessarily mean accepting the situation, although it sometimes might. More fundamentally, it means working
within the situation to further God's will. Lovingly serving others for the
glory of the Creator, remaining true to the basics of the faith, in whatever context we find ourselves, is what God wants us to do. And this takes
courage.

The hard-won insight that spiritual freedom is "nothing else than
letting God operate within my soul without interference" sustained Ciszek for the rest of his imprisonment in the Soviet Union, and beyond.[10]
He eventually signed a false confession, not because the interrogators
broke him but because he realized it was pointless to hold out. Promptly convicted of espionage, he left the five years of solitary confinement
in Lubyanka for another ten years of hard labor in Siberia. Living conditions in the lumber and mining camps in which he served his sentence
were unimaginably brutal. Temperatures in the winter were well below
zero, and snow drifts lingered even throughout the summer months.
Barracks were badly constructed, ill-heated, and overcrowded. Food
was meager and sometimes barely palatable, and medical care was haphazard. The work—cutting timber, digging ore, putting up buildings,
clearing land—was backbreaking. And the political prisoners, of which
Ciszek was one, were continuously harassed, beaten, and sometimes
murdered by the roughhewn criminal ones with whom they shared
quarters.

Like other prisoners who survived the gulag, Ciszek learned how to
scramble for extra food, occasional medical "vacations," and easier work
details. Life was still hard, and there were a couple of times in which
Ciszek just managed to pull through by the skin of his teeth. But
throughout all those years, he served his fellow prisoners by surrepti-
tiously offering mass, hearing confessions, and giving spiritual counsel
and comfort. Acting as a priest was dangerous in the camps, but the
camps were where God had placed him and wanted him to serve. In a
way that Ciszek never could've anticipated, God fulfilled his dream of
serving as a missionary priest behind the Iron Curtain.

Ciszek's term in the camps ended in 1955. But like many political
prisoners in the Soviet Union, he was then sentenced to perpetual exile

in remote areas of the country. Required to register with local police and NKVD agents, his behavior was closely monitored. Ciszek continued serving as a priest in the several towns to which he was sent, drawing the anger of authorities in each. But he was gratified by the intense longing for God among the people that he met and served. Despite harassment from police, low-paying jobs, and sometimes miserable living conditions, he was happy.

Finally, through the intervention of Attorney General Robert Kennedy, Ciszek returned to the United States in 1963 in exchange for the return to the Soviet Union of two captured spies. He had been away from home for a quarter of a century, twenty-three of them as a prisoner in the world's eyes, but a free man in God's.

16

THEA BOWMAN

I want to love until I die

Even a common cold or a slight headache can throw us into a funk. Our bodies are so closely linked to our spirits that when physical illness strikes the one, the other is inevitably affected. In a devastating sickness, the risk of falling into emotional depression and spiritual despair is high. In the ancient world, sickness was a sign of divine displeasure and a cause for hopelessness. Many of us view illness in a similar way today. When a drawn-out or incurable illness hits us, our courage can shatter under a crushing sense of God's abandonment—or, worse, of God's wrath.

If anyone ever had reason to despair because of physical illness, it was the Franciscan nun Thea Bowman. She was stricken with cancer when she was only forty-seven and in her prime as a nationally respected leader of black Catholics and champion of racial reconciliation. When she was diagnosed, her physicians told her she had only a twenty percent chance of recovery, dismal news that could've sent her into a spiritual tailspin. But Thea, bolstered by her faith in God, determined that she would look her mortality squarely in the eye and go on as long as she could. "I want to live until I die," she said. "I want to *love* until I die."[1] And she did. Despite grueling bouts of radiation and chemotherapy that did little more than delay the spread of her cancer, she went on living and loving for six more years, all the while preaching her fundamental message of embracing diversity throughout the United States and abroad. In doing so, she taught the rest of us how to face life-threatening illness with a courage fueled by trust in God's boundless grace.

Sister Thea was born Bertha Elizabeth Bowman in 1937 in the town of Canton, Mississippi. Her father, Theon, was one of only two black physicians in the area; her mother, Mary, was a former schoolteacher who educated Bertha so well at home that she was able to skip the first grade when she started school. Economically and culturally, the Bowman household was better off than many of Canton's white ones. But as a black child in pre–civil rights Mississippi, Bertha grew up with the awareness that she and her parents were second-class citizens whose welfare depended on observing the rules of the southern caste system. "I learned survival," she recalled years later. "You learn very early on how to wear the mask. . . . I learned to guard my manner, to guard my speech, even to guard my thoughts, my feelings, my passions, and emotions."[2]

Despite the necessity of appearing properly subservient when around whites, Bertha was a well-adjusted and lively child who was adoringly nurtured by her parents and Canton's close black community. She loved going to church and listening to "the old 'uns," as she called them, tell stories and sing spirituals that wove together the biblical promise of liberation and the tragic but faith-filled experience of being black in the South. She decided while still a youngster that she wanted to be a preacher.

But first she had to find a Christian tradition that suited her. By the time she was ten, she had explored all the denominations Canton had to offer, methodically visiting Methodist, Baptist, Episcopal, Adventist, and AME churches. When she got around to the local Catholic church, Holy Child Jesus Mission, she knew immediately that this was where she belonged. "I knew," she said, "I had found that for which I had been seeking."[3] She told her Protestant parents that she wanted to become a Catholic; to their great credit they gave her their blessing. One can only wonder what they thought of their young daughter's religious precocity.

A year after becoming a Catholic, Bertha enrolled in Canton's brand-new parish school, run by the Wisconsin-based Franciscan Sisters of Perpetual Adoration. She loved the nuns who taught her, and she soon announced to her parents that she wanted to join the order, which would mean leaving Canton and traveling to the motherhouse in La Crosse, Wisconsin. Her parents, not wanting to lose their only child and believing she was too young—only fifteen—to leave home, at first refused to let her go. But a determined Bertha went on a hunger strike until they finally gave in. At the train station, right before she left for Wisconsin, her worried father tried one final time to dissuade her. "They're not going to like you up there," he sadly warned, "the only black in the middle of all the whites." "I'm going to *make* them like me," Bertha replied.[4]

It didn't take Bertha long after arriving in La Crosse to understand why her father had been reluctant to let her go. She was the only black novice in the order, the only Southerner, and the only convert. Most of the sisters, she discovered, had never even spoken to a non-Catholic or a black person, and she learned very quickly that the hand-clapping and spiritual-singing style of worship she'd grown to love in Canton was frowned upon as unseemly in the all-white and straitlaced novitiate. The nuns who taught her, although kind and well-meaning, were nevertheless products of a racially segregated society. One of them, not in the least intending to be offensive, matter-of-factly informed Bertha that black people "go to nigger heaven together with the dogs and other animals." She never doubted her vocation nor regretted her decision to leave her loved ones for a cold and alien northern town. "Still," she later admitted, "secretly, I felt very much the outsider." But at the time, she kept her loneliness to herself for the most part. Only once, in an essay written in black Southern dialect entitled "Away f'om Home," did she give voice to it. She touchingly confesses that in her dreams, she can still "heah the old folks callin'." "Sometimes I think as if I'll never make it home," she wrote. "Nossuh! I ain't complainin', but thisyere ain't like home a'tall."[5]

Hard though it was, Bertha made it through the novitiate. When she took her final vows as a Franciscan sister in 1963, she chose Thea as her religious name, in honor of both her father Theon and God (*Theos* in Greek). After teaching in Wisconsin for a couple of years—she must have seemed an exotic creature to her grammar school students there—she was delighted when her order sent her back to her old parish in Canton to teach in the school that had been so important to her as a girl. Bertha, now Sister Thea, had returned home to the more congenial South.

It was a homecoming in more ways than one. While in the cold North, Thea had gradually but deliberately shed her black religious identity to conform to the subdued style of worship expected of a Roman Catholic nun. She never wavered in her loyalty to the Church. She loved being a Catholic. But turning away from the vibrant black religious tradition she had known as a child never sat well with her, and when she returned to Canton to teach black kids, she returned to her spiritual roots. She encouraged both her fellow nuns and her students to give themselves permission to "sing, pray, clap, sway, raise their hands, [and] nod their heads" when worshipping God.[6] For the rest of her life, Thea would work to nudge what was then a relentlessly white-oriented American Catholic Church in a direction more welcoming to blacks.

Thea had always loved to sing, so much so that she often trilled along with birds when she was outside. Her favorite songs were the old spirituals, full of yearning for freedom and hope, which had emerged from the slave quarters of the Old South. To her mind, they were "a living repository of the thoughts, feelings, and will of Black Spirituality," and she wanted to make sure that they were passed on to the generation that followed hers.[7] During her time in Canton, she organized a fifty-member high school choir that performed spirituals like "Deep River" and "Go Down, Moses" and eventually cut an LP album entitled *The Voice of Negro America*. On the album, Thea chanted a message that was intended as much for the Catholic Church as the nation at large. "Listen!" she said. "Hear us! . . . Though our forefathers bent to bear the heat of the sun, the strike of the lash, the chain of slavery, we are free. No man can enslave us. We are too strong, too unafraid. . . . Listen! Hear us! We are the voice of Negro America!"[8]

Starting in 1969, Thea gave up teaching in Canton and headed north again, this time to work toward a doctorate in English at Catholic University. While there, she helped found the National Black Sisters Conference and soon made a name for herself on the lecture circuit as an expert on black spirituals, poetry, and oral tradition. It was around this time that she shook off her order's drab habit for colorful traditional African caftans and turbans. She thrilled her audiences by effortlessly intermingling snatches of gospel songs in her lectures. Blacks who heard her immediately resonated with her style of preaching, while whites were often baffled and sometimes put off. But Thea refused to change. She believed that for her people to be "fully functional" as both blacks *and* Catholics, the predominantly white Church had to learn to accept them as they are. "I bring myself, my black self, all that I am, all that I have . . . my African-American song and dance and gesture and movement and teaching and preaching and healing and responsibility as gift to the church."[9]

During the turbulent civil rights movement of the 1960s, some black leaders had advocated assimilation as the surest route to social equality while other more militant ones insisted that whites and blacks could never coexist peacefully. Thea rejected both of these positions. She had little use for melting pot solutions to racial tensions, believing that it was vital that each ethnic or religious group retain its unique identity. People are different, she taught, and their differences ought to be celebrated rather than artificially washed away. But by the same token, using racial identity as a bludgeon was no solution either. All human beings are kin to one another by virtue of their common divine Parent. "The very word 'catholic,'" she was fond of reminding her fellow Catholics, "means 'all.' Jesus loved all men—and true love always tends to bring people together." So while Thea enthusiastically proclaimed that "Black is beautiful!" she didn't stop there. "White is beautiful! Brown is beautiful! Red is beautiful! Yellow is beautiful! All the colors and hues in between that God made us are beautiful! Straight hair is beautiful! Kinky hair is beautiful! Bald is beautiful!"[10]

Thea joined the faculty of Viterbo University after she earned her PhD in 1972. She taught there for six years, becoming one of the institution's most popular professors. But in 1978 she returned to Canton. Her parents were old and frail, and she felt the need to be closer to them. Soon after her arrival, the far-sighted bishop of Mississippi asked her to serve as the diocese's director of intercultural awareness. It was a perfect job for someone with Thea's interests and talents, and for the rest of her life she spoke at churches, universities, schools, and civic groups across the nation about the reconciling love offered by Christ that embraces rather than rejects diversity. Love, she insisted over and over, was the key. "Loving ground becomes holy ground; holy ground becomes Kingdom ground."[11]

Thea turned forty-seven in 1984. It turned out to be a bad year for her. In March, she was diagnosed with breast cancer that had metastasized, and she began a course of chemotherapy so brutal that she eventually discontinued it, opting instead for radiation treatment. By mid-1985, she'd had so many treatments that she laughingly called herself a "certified radiant woman." Thea would always look for what humor she could throughout the entire course of her illness. A few years later, when a resumed course of chemotherapy caused her hair to fall out, she joked with audiences that her grooming ritual was now much easier: "one swipe with a damp washcloth and a touch of oil for sheen."[12]

Toward the end of the same year in which she was diagnosed, Thea's aged parents died within weeks of one another. Their passing was a double blow, but Thea took comfort in the fact that they were spared worrying about the outcome of her illness. Like so many other cancer patients, Thea discovered that one of the hardest things about being desperately sick is the emotional burden it inflicts on loved ones.

Although her treatments horribly drained her strength and resources, they managed to stall the spread of her cancer. Thea was in remission by the end of 1985, and would remain that way for a couple of years. Before falling ill, she had always assumed she'd live long enough to become an "old 'un" herself. But afterward, even while in remission, she sensed that her time was short, and in her talks around the country began stressing even more than before the importance of lovingly celebrating the diversity of God's people. Life, she now appreciated, was fragile and fleeting, far too short, even for healthy persons, to waste any of it by not loving as fully as one could. As for herself, she wanted to expand the orbit of her love as widely as possible before the end. Tempting as it must've been at times to give herself over to despair, she wanted to keep on loving until she died.

The capacity for giving and receiving love becomes all important to someone facing a serious, much less fatal, disease. But, tragically, the capacity sometimes dries up. When we find ourselves up against the terminus of our days, especially if our interior resources are buffeted by increasing waves of pain and debility, there is a tendency either to withdraw from the world, including from those we love, or to clutch desperately at family, friends, physicians, and acquaintances in a panicked effort to hold back the fear and loneliness of dying. The first response isolates us from others by locking us inside our own grief. We become too self-absorbed to give or receive love. The second isn't a gesture of love so much as frantic need in which we reach out to others not to give ourselves to them so much as to use them as life buoys. In either case, love gets drowned in the kind of hopeless misery that leads to spiritual despair.

But Thea, despite the incredible suffering she endured when the cancer returned two years before her death, managed to avoid tumbling into this abyss. She was too dedicated to encouraging others to "open up to life," which for her always meant opening up to love, to obsess over her own fate. She wasn't indifferent to what was happening to her. Like all of us, she wanted to live a long, healthy, and happy life. But the same love that had given her the courage to endure segregation in the South of her childhood, loneliness in the novitiate, and the Church's indifference to her black spiritual heritage, also gave her the courage to continue serving others even as her own life was slipping away from her. To keep on keeping on, she said, was a lesson she learned from the "old 'uns." "Old people in the black community taught us that we should serve the Lord on our deathbeds or in any circumstances in life. If we have faith, hope and love we can pass it on."[13]

By January 1988, Thea's cancer had returned, this time invading her spine and bones. Radiation was no longer an option, so she returned to chemotherapy, despite the nausea, dizziness, thrush, and weakness it brought. The malignancy made her bones so brittle that she soon had to rely on a wheelchair lest she fall and shatter herself. There would be no remission this time.

Bone cancer is a particularly painful and merciless carcinoma. When the physical torture became too unbearable for Thea, she tried to distract herself by singing the old black spirituals she had learned to love as a child. And when she hadn't the strength for even that, she moaned the songs as best she could. Music, she said, allowed her to continue praying and provided her with a way of uniting herself to God. Finally, after months of suffering, Thea returned to God in March 1990. Her gravestone was engraved with an epitaph she had written herself. "She tried."

Throughout her years of lecturing on racial reconciliation and celebrating diversity, Thea broke into a tune so frequently that it became her signature song. It was "This Little Light of Mine," a spiritual that became popular in the 1920s. It's a catchy although slightly corny song, expressing a message dearly loved by Thea: love is the light that illuminates the world and holds back the darkness of spiritual despair. This is because the "little light" of human love is fueled by the divine light of Love before which no secret is hidden, no anxiety is unnoticed, and no fear can withstand. In her living, and especially in her dying, Thea

Bowman strove to let her light, and God's, "shine, shine, shine." In doing so she demonstrated the truth that love is as strong as death.

17

C. S. LEWIS

how many hours in a mile?

C. S. Lewis once told a friend that he was given late in life what had been denied him in his youth: romantic love. When he was nearly sixty, he fell in love with an American poet named Joy Davidman. His marriage to her changed his life in ways he couldn't have imagined.

Lewis and Davidman met in 1952. A wife and mother of two young sons, Davidman was a convert to Christianity and admirer of Lewis's books who traveled to England to make his acquaintance. Lewis was impressed by her poetry and amused by her wit. But he kept her at arm's length.

Davidman, however, had much stronger feelings for Lewis. So when her troubled marriage finally ended a few months after her initial trip to England, she decided to pull up stakes and move there permanently. With her two boys in tow, she rented a flat first in London and then in Oxford. Lewis, who by that time considered her a friend but apparently nothing more, helped her out from time to time with small sums of cash. He also wrote a preface to the British edition of her *Smoke on the Mountain*, a study of the Ten Commandments, that considerably boosted its sales. Finally, he became a friend and confidant to her two sons, even though it took some time for the lifelong bachelor to acclimate to children. As he wryly wrote a friend after one excursion with the boys, "I never knew what we celibates are shielded from. I will never laugh at parents again. Not that the boys weren't a delight: but a delight like surf-bathing which leaves one breathless and aching. The energy, the tempo, is what kills."[1]

Lewis's willingness to help out Davidman and her sons jumped to a whole new level in the spring of 1956. The British government declined to renew her visa, probably because she had been an active communist when she was younger, and she was faced with the prospect of deportation. Davidman desperately wanted to stay in the country. To help her out in her trouble, Lewis quietly married her in a short civil ceremony. He insisted at the time that the marriage was nothing more than a legal expediency, and afterward the two continued living separately. But in hindsight, it's likely that Lewis's feelings for Davidman around this time began to mature from affection to love, even if he wasn't yet ready to admit it.

The boundary of their relationship changed abruptly in October 1956 when Davidman, who had taken a tumble in her flat and broken a leg, was discovered while in hospital to have bone cancer. Doctors thought it unlikely that she could survive, and the prospect of losing her brought home to Lewis the depth of his feelings. He both declared his love and faithfully attended her over the next few months as she endured several surgeries and radiation treatments. In March of the following year, warned by doctors that she hadn't much longer to live, Lewis determined to wed her in a proper religious ceremony. He had some difficulty finding an Anglican priest who would officiate. At the time, the Church of England forbade divorced people to remarry, and even priests who disagreed with the prohibition were reluctant to risk the wrath of their bishops. But Lewis eventually located a sympathetic priest, and he and Davidman, fully expecting that their time together as man and wife would be brief, were wed. Lewis took her out of hospital to the Oxfordshire cottage he shared with his brother Warnie. He wanted her to die at home.

And then the miracle—for so the two considered it—happened: Davidman's cancer went into what appeared to be spontaneous remission. Within a few weeks the ominous dark spots on her x-rays shrank, her strength returned, and she was hobbling about the garden on crutches. A few more weeks and she had the energy to supervise the redecoration of the cottage (much to the annoyance of Warnie, who intensely disliked changes) and eventually to travel to Wales, Ireland, and Greece with Lewis. Although some of Lewis's Oxford colleagues and friends who disapproved of the marriage cut the couple from their social circle, he and Davidman were blissfully content. But the idyll ended all too soon. In October 1959, a routine medical checkup revealed that her cancer had returned with a vengeance, and in six months, two years after her deathbed marriage to Lewis, Davidman succumbed. She was barely forty-five, and the final days of her life were unspeakably painful. She died screaming in agony.

Davidman's death was shocking enough for Lewis, but the suffering she endured toward the end sent him positively reeling with grief and dismay. For the first time since his conversion to Christianity in 1932, the God he had written about with such confidence in so many books had suddenly become alien and menacing. It wasn't that his wife's death had pushed him into atheism. No, he was still a believer. Now, however, his anger over the agony Davidman had endured led him to suspect that God, far from being loving and compassionate, was the "Cosmic Sadist, the spiteful imbecile," who tortures humans for the sheer fun of it.[2] In his crushing grief, Lewis felt himself sinking into a dark despair which made everything he had once believed and proclaimed, loudly and at times even pugnaciously, look shabby and false.

Lewis recorded his spiritual crisis in a little memoir modestly but appropriately entitled *A Grief Observed*. Although not as widely read as his apologetic works or his novels, *A Grief Observed* is by far his best book. It records the story of a man who courageously faced one of the worst things that can happen, the painful death of a loved one. Lewis's battle with despair didn't culminate in a Hollywoodish happy ending. It left him a wounded, sobered man who carried the grief of his wife's death to his own grave three years later. But in breaking open his heart, it *did* make him more sensitive to the world's pain and more alert to the unfathomable mysteriousness of God. His descent into darkness broke him, but the break made him a better man and a wiser Christian.

A central theme in *A Grief Observed* is absence or void, the experience of which Lewis found to be unbearably palpable. Initially surprised that his grief over his wife's death felt so much like fear, he soon realized that all grief evokes a primordial dread of absence, or nonbeing. In the void left by a departed loved one, the entire universe hemorrhages meaning, leaving the mourner in a coldly desolate moonscape stripped of human as well as divine companionship, burdened by a haunting sense that the bottom has dropped out of things.

The most immediate void endured by the bereft person is, of course, the beloved who has died. After Davidman's death, Lewis discovered that her absence saturated every place he went. "Her absence is like the sky, spread over everything," he noted in bewilderment. "Is anything more certain than that in all those vast times and spaces, if I were allowed to search them, I should nowhere find her face, her voice, her touch?"[3] Even more devastatingly, Lewis realized that with the passing of days and weeks, absence had begun to infect his personal memories of Davidman as well. They were slowly but inexorably disappearing under a snowfall of his own expectations and impressions and heart-ache, until he feared that the only mental image of her left him would be one he had selectively recast. He knew that a single encounter with the "rough, sharp, cleansing tang of her otherness" would sweep away his illusory memories.[4] But this, of course, was impossible.

Lewis's despair over his wife's absence was compounded by the sickening suspicion that the loving and compassionate God he had wor-shipped was in fact a delusion, and that he had been a fool ever to suppose otherwise. Desperate questions boiled in his mind. Why would a good God give humans life only to snatch it away? Why were his prayers for his wife's health ignored? Why did God allow her to die in such physical agony? The silence of God—the *absence* of God—was as inexplicable as it was dreadful. When you're happy and content, Lewis noted, God seems to be perpetually present. But if you turn to him in a dark and hopeless moment, needing his presence more than ever, what do you find? Void. Absence. "A door slammed in your face, and a sound of bolting and double bolting on the inside. After that, silence. You may as well turn away."[5]

What Lewis was wrestling with in his crushing grief was a puzzle that has plagued humankind for millennia: why would a good God allow evil to befall innocent people? Either God is powerless to prevent it, or he doesn't care to prevent it. Whichever alternative is the correct one, humans come out on the short end of the stick. Lewis believed that the demolition of his world wrought by his wife's death had finally opened his eyes to the absurdity of believing that God cared for human welfare, and this harsh and terrible conclusion nearly destroyed him. His broth-er Warnie and his many friends and acquaintances, even those who had shaken their heads and tsked when he married the outspoken American divorcee, feared for his sanity and his life. That he held on to both during this nightmarish period wasn't an act of will on his part. He was too stunned by the dark night into which Davidman's death and God's absence had thrust him to be capable of self-direction. What kept him going was sheer inertia and, he later realized, grace.

Finally, after weeks of restless nights and benumbed days, a breakthrough occurred. It suddenly came to him that perhaps the universe might not be so desolately empty after all. It was an intuition rather than a full-blown, defensible argument—and if ever a man loved rigorous thinking, it was Lewis—so the only way he knew how to express it was through simile.

> Imagine a man in total darkness. He thinks he is in a cellar or dungeon. Then there comes a sound. He thinks it might be a sound from far off—waves or wind-blown trees or cattle half a mile away. And if so, it proves he's not in a cellar, but free, in the open air. Or it may be a much smaller sound close at hand—a chuckle of laughter. And if so, there is a friend just beside him in the dark. Either way, a good, good sound.[6]

Lewis was never able to put his finger on what had happened in that breakthrough moment to hint that the absence that had haunted him since his wife's death wasn't comprehensive, and that despite the very real desolation there was the chance of a companionable and liberating presence. No one would've blamed him had he dismissed the experience as a bit of wishful thinking prompted by desperate loneliness. But he chose to see it as a real sign that in fact the universe wasn't empty or indifferent, and that God wasn't the Cosmic Sadist. It's in this resolve to be steadfastly loyal to the possibility that life could be meaningful after the beloved's death that Lewis displayed spiritual courage. He could've sunk deeper into his despair; that, in fact, would've been the easier way to go, requiring no effort to let the dark waters close over his head. But instead he held fast to the first sign of renewal offered him, as Jacob clutched the angel and refused to let go until he got a blessing.

Thinking back over the weeks of despair that preceded the breakthrough, Lewis realized that some of the dreadful absence he had endured was caused by the intensity of his own grief. He had failed to see any way out of the void because his suffering had blinded and deafened him. "Passionate grief," he discovered, "does not link us with the dead but cuts us off from them."[7] The moment he quieted down, probably out of sheer weariness, the snowflakes that were covering over his memories of Joy began to melt.

As for God's apparent absence, Lewis concluded that it had been his "own frantic need that slammed" the divine door in his face.[8] He had kicked and hammered at the door with such desperate frenzy that he'd drowned out any response God might have offered him. God wasn't silent, and never had been. He just wasn't saying what Lewis wanted to hear. Lewis had wanted God to rush in, speak some comforting platitudes, and fix the horrible situation in which he found himself in the wake of Davidman's death. In his grief he had prayed to have her with him again, even if only for a few moments, even if it meant that she would have to go through the ordeal of dying all over again. But now he recognized both the selfishness of his prayer as well as the childishly magical way of thinking about God that lay behind it. Both were delusions that only thrust him more deeply into despair.

What Lewis came to realize in coming to terms with the loss of the woman he loved was that his notion of God had been largely a flimsy house of cards, ready to tumble at the slightest of tremors, much less the tectonic shift of being widowed. Just as his memories of his wife had been insidiously snowflaked by his own needs, so his magical understanding of God was likewise a self-serving fiction tested and found wanting by tragedy. Even after this dawned on him, Lewis sometimes found himself yearning for the old Fixer God. Hardened habits and engrained needs don't die easily. But each time he tried to rebuild the house of cards, the divine iconoclast found a way to knock it down, just as he had when he took Davidman away.

In arriving at this conclusion, Lewis knew that he was balancing on a razor's edge. It's one thing to say that God, for our own good, periodically demolishes our illusions and self-deceptions. It's quite another to say that God does so by inflicting suffering and death on our loved ones. True, Lewis never quite said that God killed Davidman to teach him a lesson, but he came disconcertingly close at times. What ultimately held him back was the conviction there was little distinction between a God who would torture the innocent as an object lesson for onlookers, and the Cosmic Sadist. Believing that God had allowed Joy to die in order to test and improve Lewis's faith might've infused a semblance of meaning into her death, but it would've also meant building another house of cards.

So in the end, Lewis bowed to something that as a scholar and robust Christian apologist he had always mightily resisted. He admitted that his mind was too finite, too human, to fathom the ways of God. Just like the biblical Job, Lewis acknowledged that he couldn't explain away the reality of innocent suffering in the world with slick theological arguments (as he had tried to do, for example, in his 1940 *The Problem of Pain*). Nor would it do to petulantly shake a fist at God for not preventing evil. Innocent suffering like that endured by his wife was simply too vast a mystery for him, or any other human, to grasp. As he confessed, "Five senses; an incurably abstract intellect; a haphazardly selective memory; a set of preconceptions and assumptions so numerous that I can never examine more than a minority of them—never become conscious of them all. How much of total reality can such an apparatus let through?"[9] Evil existed. Bad things happened to good people, despite the existence of an all-powerful and all-loving God. But demanding to know why necessarily brought only silence—not the silence of a haughty, uncaring God, but that of a compassionate one who knows that the question is unanswerable because it's nonsensical. It's tantamount to asking "How many hours are there in a mile?" or "Is yellow square or round?"[10] What reasonable person would expect an answer?

Lewis survived his wife by a bit more than three years. But friends noticed that he was more subdued than he had once been, less ready to engage in exuberant religious debates, more tentative in his assertions. Readers who had come to expect a steady flow of books from him were disappointed. Lewis no longer felt the need to scribble as obsessively as he had before Davidman's death. It was almost as if he were marking time until he could join her.

The final years of Lewis's life seemed, on the surface, to be ones of quiet resignation. But actually they were testaments to a courageous resolve on his part to trust in God despite the blow that had shattered the house of cards on which he'd pinned all his earlier hopes. Almost a year to the day before he died, Lewis wrote a letter to a Mrs. Arnold that gives some idea of what had been taken from him and the courage it took to endure its loss. "By nature," he wrote, "I demand from the arrangements of this world just that permanence which God has expressly refused to give me."

I would like everything to be immemorial—to have the same old horizons, the same garden, the same smells and sounds, always there, changeless. The old wine is to me always better. That is, I desire the "abiding city" where I well know it is not and ought not to be found. I suppose all these changes should prepare us for the greater change which has drawn nearer even since I began this letter. We must "sit light" not only to life itself but to all its phases. The useless word is "encore."[11]

18

HENRI NOUWEN

to choose not death, but life

The book that made Henri Nouwen famous, *The Wounded Healer,* was published when he was still a relatively young man. It was a psychological and pastoral reflection on how crucial it is for pastors to touch and acknowledge their own wounds if they hope to relate to the suffering of their parishioners. At the time, and even today in some quarters, the standard conviction was that clergy had to be invincibly strong, never showing weakness to others or even themselves, to do their job effectively. *The Wounded Healer* exposed that way of thinking for the damaging myth it is.

Nouwen's book was the first in what became a long series of psychological, spiritual, and theological insights on the role of suffering in shaping human identity and informing our relationship to God. From Nouwen's perspective, all of us are born with a deep and abiding loneliness. We yearn to love and to be loved, and if that craving goes unfulfilled, we live in anguish. But the anguish, if heeded, can also draw us closer to precisely what we so desperately want. Within our very wounds lies the secret of our healing.

This was no abstract theorizing on Nouwen's part. Throughout his entire adult life, he wrestled with a deep fear, one he was never totally able to shake, that he was unworthy of love. It made him restless, too hard on himself, and sometimes too needy in his relationships with others. It eventually hurled him into a six-month period of spiritual despair which nearly destroyed him. As he said at the time in a secretly kept journal, he felt a deep hole in his being where love should've been, and he recognized that the hole could never be filled because his needs were "inexhaustible." But from the depths of his despair, he mustered the spiritual courage to confront his loneliness and learn from it. "There are two extremes to avoid," he came to realize, "being completely absorbed in your pain and being distracted by so many things that you stay far away from the wound you want to heal."[1] Up to the time of his collapse, he had tried to flee the pain, and during its worst moments he had nearly drowned in it. But afterward, in a move he never could've anticipated, he found himself grateful for it.

Henri Nouwen was born in central Holland on January 24, 1932; propitiously for a future author, it was the Feast of St. Francis de Sales, the patron of writers. The household in which he was raised was deeply Catholic, and while still a youngster, Henri declared his intention to become a priest. He entered minor seminary when he was eighteen—he had wanted to enter four years earlier, but his father thought him too young and vetoed the idea—and was ordained seven years later. His bishop intended to send him to Rome's Gregorian University for graduate work in theology, but young Father Nouwen asked permission to study psychology at the Dutch Catholic University instead. For the next seven years he received training in clinical psychology, with a special emphasis on pastoral counseling.

In 1964, Nouwen traveled to Topeka, Kansas, to study for two years at the Menninger Clinic, a pioneering psychiatric treatment center. While there, he discovered the work of Anton Boisen, founder of the clinical pastoral education movement that has become a mainstay in the training of American clergy. Boisen argued that it was important for seminarians to spend time in hospitals ministering to people in mental and physical distress. Not only was this valuable hands-on experience for future pastors, priests, and rabbis, but it also showed them, Boisen hoped, aspects of the human/divine relationship that otherwise might go unnoticed. Patients in crisis, he taught, especially psychiatric ones, were often closer to God than healthy and complacent persons.

Nouwen met Boisen when the latter was an old and somewhat confused man close to death. He was struck by the realization that it was through Boisen's *own* wounds—the elder man had a long history of mental illness—that he had gained his fundamental insights. Nouwen learned through his encounter with Boisen "how a deep wound can become a source of beauty in which even the weaknesses seem to give light."[2] This would be the fundamental insight that inspired his own creative work for the rest of his life.

After his training at the Menninger Clinic, Nouwen launched an academic career. He spent a few years as a professor at Notre Dame and a couple more as head of behavioral sciences at Utrecht's Catholic Theological Institute before accepting a position at Yale Divinity School. During the decade he spent there, Nouwen mentored dozens of students, many of whom went on to make names for themselves as theologians or pastors, and became one of the campus's most popular teachers and beloved counselors. Churning out at least one book a year, most of them wildly popular, he also began to gain an international reputation as a writer on Christian spirituality.

But underneath his success as a teacher, author, and spiritual director, Nouwen was a troubled man. Although he had grown up in a richly nurturing family, as a child he had needed constant affirmation from his parents and siblings. This need continued into adulthood, becoming even more acute as he wrestled with the loneliness of priestly celibacy as well as the sense of moral failure that began to haunt him when he admitted to himself, probably during his time at the Menninger Clinic, that he was a homosexual. For most of his life, his loneliness and insecurity drove him to try to earn the love and approval of others through his writing.

They also bred a restlessness in Nouwen that displayed in his sometimes frenetic search for a vocation in which he could feel at home. During his years at Yale, he spent two six-month sabbaticals, one in 1974 and the other in 1979, at Trappist monasteries, observing the cycle of prayer with the cloistered monks, testing whether God wanted him to join them permanently. Resigning from Yale in 1981, he flew to Lima, Peru, to work with Maryknoll priests and nuns in the barrios, discerning whether missionary work was his calling. Concluding that it wasn't, he returned to the United States early the next year to accept an appointment at Harvard Divinity School. His monastic and South American experiments hadn't brought him the sense of completion or belonging he longed for any more than his time at Yale had. But he decided to give academia another try.

It was perhaps the biggest mistake of his life, because Harvard was exactly the wrong environment for a man already suffering from a lonely sense of inadequacy. Although well-known as an author, Nouwen didn't have a doctorate or strong academic credentials, and this soon made him feel the odd man out in the highly competitive atmosphere of one of the world's most prestigious universities. Moreover, his teaching style was viewed with suspicion by many of his fellow professors as well as some of his students. Nouwen always wanted to make his courses spiritual as well as intellectual experiences. He worried that seminary training, especially at high-powered educational institutions, tended to educate the head at the expense of the heart. So he typically began each class session by asking students to join him in meditative Taizé chants. His more buttoned-down colleagues disapproved, and he found himself shunned socially and academically. After four years of feeling rejected at Harvard, Nouwen's inner turmoil and gnawing loneliness had been primed to an unbearable level. When he resigned in 1985, neither he nor his colleagues regretted his going.

Academia, missionary work, and monastic contemplation hadn't been where Nouwen belonged. So after leaving Harvard, he struck out into what for him were totally uncharted waters. He flew to Trosly, France, to live and work for a time in the L'Arche community there. The year he spent in France would usher in both the breakdown that nearly destroyed him and a new ministry that fulfilled him more than any other had.

L'Arche was founded in 1964 by Jean Vanier, an ex-naval officer who resigned his commission in 1950, earned a PhD at the Sorbonne, and opened up a faith-based home for intellectually disabled adults. Vanier, like Anton Boisen, was convinced that the wounds humans suffer can draw them nearer to God, and that their caretakers in turn can be blessed by them. Jesus told his disciples that he could be found in all those marginalized or rejected by society. What better place to seek Jesus, therefore, than in, with, and through the intellectually challenged?

Nouwen's experience at Trosly brought him into close contact with people—the disabled residents of the house—who had absolutely no knowledge of his books or his reputation and so weren't impressed by his celebrity status. If they accepted him, they did so because of the man he was, not the reputation as a spiritual author he had acquired. For a basically insecure man like Nouwen who had always felt he had to prove himself, this was an utterly unfamiliar and disturbing situation to be in. Unshielded as he was by his public persona, he was forced to ask himself fundamental questions about his identity, his fears, and his hopes, and to do so in an environment full of handicapped people who required his help, sometimes literally to go to the bathroom. The author of *The Wounded Healer* was thrown, for the first time in his life, into a situation in which his own carefully avoided wounds now clamored for attention.

Nouwen's way of dealing with them wasn't healthy. He tried to protect himself from the loneliness deep inside him by falling desperately in love with a young L'Arche coworker named Nathan Ball. Although Nouwen never for a moment contemplated betraying his priestly celibacy, the turmoil into which the past few years had thrown him now erupted in a frank self-acknowledgment of his homosexuality, and for the first time in his life he allowed himself to love another man romantically. But given his emotional state, the love was too based on need to be healthy or fruitful. Nouwen became obsessed with Ball, overdemanding and needy, causing the younger man, who didn't share Nouwen's romantic interest, to withdraw. Ball's perfectly understandable refusal to reciprocate his affection only added to the already tormented Nouwen's sense of loneliness and rejection.

Realizing he needed to get away from what had become for him a toxic situation, Nouwen relocated to Daybreak, a L'Arche community in Canada, where he planned to serve as chaplain. But he soon realized that the demons he tried to leave behind in France had pursued him to North America, and by December 1987 he had collapsed. "Everything came crashing down," he recalled, "my self-esteem, my energy to live and work, my sense of being loved, my hope for healing, my trust in God—everything." He had come, he later realized, "face to face with my own nothingness. It was as if all that had given my life meaning was pulled away." He teetered before "a bottomless abyss."[3]

It soon became clear that Nouwen, who wept constantly and refused consolation, company, and food, needed professional help. He was packed off to an institution where he received pastoral and spiritual counseling twice a day for six months. At the end of that time, he returned to the Daybreak community. He had managed "to enter the basement of my soul and look directly at what was hidden there": the loneliness, the yearning for acceptance and love, the dread of not being welcomed by either his fellow humans or by God unless he somehow wowed them with his accomplishments. And in entering the basement, he was empowered to "choose, in the face of it all, not death but life."[4]

Nouwen's characterization of his breakdown as a time in which he stood before a "bottomless abyss" is revealing, because it's reminiscent of something he had written years earlier in *The Wounded Healer.* He wrote that loneliness inflicted a wound on humans "like the Grand Canyon—a deep incision in the surface of our existence." It takes great courage to dare to lean over and peer into the depths of the incision. But if one steels oneself to look, the abyss can reveal "an inexhaustible source of beauty and self-understanding."[5] This is precisely what Nouwen discovered, years after he wrote these words, during his recovery. Sometimes the longest journey in the world is the one from the head to the heart.

What happened? What brought Nouwen to the breakthrough that eventually allowed him to see his own suffering as a source of beauty and insight rather than a demon to be feared and avoided?

Thanks to the patient counseling he received during his six-month crisis, Nouwen came to realize that he had lived as a spiritual coward for most of his life, adamantly refusing to acknowledge what was really driving his suffering. He had convinced himself that his pain was caused from being rejected by others, including God. But once he gazed into the Grand Canyon of his soul, he was able to discern that it wasn't others who rejected him. Instead, he had rejected himself, and then projected the rejection as coming from external sources. His wounds were real, but they were mainly self-inflicted.

Ultimately, Nouwen realized, he had rejected himself, and then convinced himself that everyone else had as well, because he believed himself unlovable. The roots of this conviction are undoubtedly tangled and hard to unravel, but certainly a significant one was the guilt and, at least for a time, the self-loathing he felt for his sexual orientation. Nouwen was in many ways a very traditional Roman Catholic. He celebrated mass every day of his life after his ordination, he never publicly disagreed with his religious superiors, he valued clerical celibacy, and he accepted unquestioningly for many years the Church's moral condemnation of homosexuality. So on top of the other sources of his sense of inadequacy was added the guilt of an "unnatural" attraction to men. Even toward the end of his life, after he'd moved toward a personal acceptance of his sexual orientation, he resisted the urging of a few friends to come out for fear that doing so might somehow damage the Church.

Nouwen's intense suffering brought with it the realization that both his self-rejection and sense of being rejected by others, based as they were on his deep fear of being unlovable, were avoidable once he came to grips with the fact that he was both lovable and loved. He grew into the awareness of what he called the First Love: God's love for God's creation, a love that may at times be disappointed but never diminishes, much less ceases. Nouwen, like every human who has ever lived, was loved by God even while he was still in the womb. Nouwen, like every creature made by God, was inherently lovable because stamped with the seal of the supremely lovable God who brought him into being.

Given the easiness with which we humans fall into guilty self-hatred, this First Love, which "precedes all human love," is often difficult to believe in or to accept. For many of us, and certainly for Nouwen, doing so requires an act of trust that doesn't come easily. It requires courage—the courage needed to look into the abyss and see the wound for what it actually is instead of what one assumes it to be. But when the courage is mustered and the trust is placed, one realizes that the loneliness which all humans experience from time to time, the sense of emptiness and unfulfilled yearning, isn't the "final experience," but "that beyond it is a place where you are held in love."[6] Knowing that, one is able to cope with the pain, and just as importantly, is in a better position to help others cope with theirs. One becomes a wounded healer because, as Nouwen says, the pain that earlier threatened to destroy has now been called home, incorporated into the self, and is now ready to "bear fruit in your heart and the hearts of others."[7]

Finding the courage to face the truth about his sense of inadequacy and to trust in the First Love rejuvenated Nouwen. He was able to reestablish the friendship with Nathan Ball that his earlier neediness had sundered, and when he returned to Daybreak, his relationship with the residents there was more caring, compassionate, and giving. Nouwen had discovered that the pain which had broken his heart, when entered into deeply enough to reveal the First Love, also allowed his heart to open wide enough to relate more authentically to the pain of others.

It's not surprising that after his crisis, Nouwen became fascinated with trapeze artists on the one hand and Rembrandt's famous painting of the Prodigal Son's return to his father on the other. Finding the courage to trust that one is God's beloved, Nouwen discovered, is a bit like performing on the high wire: you have to resist the temptation to grasp at the catcher's hands as you're flying through the air toward him. If you try to grab him, you'll wind up breaking your wrists and tumbling to the ground. You simply have to trust that he'll catch you, just as you have to trust that God loves you.

The story of the Prodigal Son, both the parable in Luke's gospel and Rembrandt's painting, spoke to the same issue. Nouwen had long been captivated by them. After finding the courage to accept the First Love, he knew why. Both had been telling him the truth about his own situation all along, despite the fact that he obstinately refused to listen. The Prodigal Son could've returned home at any time to be enfolded by the embrace of a loving father. But he had stayed away out of shame and guilt, convinced that he was no longer lovable and no longer loved. It took a great act of courage for him to finally return home and throw himself at his father's feet. But in doing so, he discovered that he had always been loved and would always be loved. And with that happy realization, the Prodigal Son, and of course Nouwen, chose life instead of death.

19

MOTHER TERESA

I will be a saint of darkness

In 2007, a book appeared that shocked many. It was a compilation of letters written by Mother Teresa, founder and head of the Missionaries of Charity, which revealed that for the last fifty years of her life, with the exception of but a single month, she suffered from a spiritual emptiness that made her feel utterly abandoned by God. "This untold darkness," she wrote in 1961, "this continual longing for God—He does not want me—He is not there."[1]

Some people, most often long-standing critics of Teresa's, were quick to blast her as a hypocrite and fraud who had put on a pious face for the sake of raking in donations and fame. But even her admirers were bewildered by the news that a woman they venerated as holy—and one, moreover, fast-tracked for sainthood by Pope John Paul II—should in fact have been unable, by her own admission, to pray for the greater part of her adult life. What were they supposed to think now?

Both responses are understandable. Yet those who charged Mother Teresa with hypocrisy as well as those confused or disappointed by her confessed alienation from God missed the deeper significance of her ordeal. Teresa's lonely aching for God all those years revealed in her a spiritual courage that is as astounding as it is inspiring. Despite ample opportunity to sink into despair and turn away from the work to which she had been called, Teresa chose instead to cleave to God, absent though God seemed, and eventually to accept her pain as a participation in Christ's own suffering. In enduring the abandonment, she offered up the only thing she had left to give: steadfastness.

Given the intensity of her devotion during her first thirty-five years, the agony of Teresa's subsequent sense of God's absence is all the more poignant. Born Gonxha Agnes Bojaxhiu into a devout Albanian family, she joined the Ireland-based Sisters of Loreto in 1928 when she was only eighteen, determined to devote her life to God. Three months later, she found herself teaching at one of the order's schools in India, a task that she threw herself into with gusto for nearly two decades. She took her religious name in honor of the "Little Flower," Thérèse of Lisieux, the Carmelite nun who famously wrote that one can serve God in "little ways"—going about one's daily chores, for example, while practicing the presence of God—just as conscientiously as in "big" ones. Some time after taking her public vows of obedience, chastity, and poverty, Mother Teresa made a private one to Jesus, swearing to deny him nothing and to give him all. "Why must we give ourselves fully to God?" she once wrote. "Because God has given Himself to us. . . . I live for God and give up my own self, and in this way induce God to live for me. Therefore to possess God we must allow Him to possess our soul."[2] Years later, Teresa would discover that the consequences of this private vow to give Jesus all were much more complicated than she could've imagined when she made it.

A turning point for Teresa occurred quite unexpectedly. She was on a train traveling from Calcutta to Darjeeling, headed for a religious retreat, when she had an intense vision of Christ asking her to forsake her ministry with the Loreto Sisters and dedicate the rest of her life to serving the poorest of the poor. Teresa never talked much about the experience, but when she did she always referred to it as her "call within a call." God, she believed, had offered her "an invitation to perfect the vocation that he had given to me when I was eighteen. . . . I needed to leave the convent and live with the poor." Christ also revealed to Teresa that by "the poor" he meant "the most miserable, the poorest of the poor in Calcutta": those who are abandoned, infested with parasites, too naked to beg in public, too weak from starvation to even chew food, and too sick to live. "These are the people," she said, "that Jesus, during that trip, told me to love."[3] From Teresa's perspective, ministering to these unfortunates was simultaneously a response to Jesus's cry "I thirst!" from the Cross.

But the wheels of the Church turn slowly. To follow her call within a call, Teresa knew that she would have to leave the Loreto Sisters and found a new religious order dedicated to living with and ministering to the poorest of the poor, and for that she needed her bishop's approval. Her vision of Christ occurred in September 1946. She would have to wait until January 1948 before she finally got the green light from her superiors. Once the go-ahead was received, she moved into a Calcutta slum and soon became well known in the neighborhood as someone who was ready to help others, even though she herself was so poor that she sometimes had to beg for her daily food. Over the next two years, as word of her ministry spread, several women joined her to form a community of caregivers who lived, prayed, and worked together. Soon, as more women joined, other houses dedicated to serving the poor sprang up throughout Calcutta. In October 1950, the Vatican officially approved of the ministry, and the Congregation of the Missionaries of Charity was formally chartered. In two more years, the order opened its first hospice, followed quickly by hospitals for lepers and homes for orphans whose parents had died on the streets. Eventually, missions were established in North America, Asia, and Europe, and Mother Teresa became an internationally recognized figure beloved by millions, honored by world leaders, and consulted by popes.

The success of the Missionaries of Charity was dramatic. In the eyes of the world, God seemed to have favored Teresa and her vision. But for her personally, a terrible darkness had set in shortly—and ironically—after she embarked on her new ministry. She kept her spiritual despair mainly to herself, putting on a good face for the sake of the work and her fellow nuns. Over the years, she admitted her anguish to only a handful of confessors. But inside, she felt spiritually dead. In a plea to God that she wrote in 1959, she expressed her agony in terms that are painful to read. "Alone. The darkness is so dark—and I am alone.—Unwanted, forsaken.—The loneliness of the heart that wants love is unbearable.—Where is my faith?—even deep down, right in, there is nothing but emptiness & darkness." To compound her misery, she began to feel dishonest about hiding her dryness from her sisters, even though she did so out of concern for them. "The whole time smiling," she wrote. "Sisters & people . . . they think my faith, trust & love are filling my very being & that the intimacy with God and union to His will must be absorbing my heart.—Could they but know."[4] But she also feared that going public would refocus attention away from Jesus and onto her.

In a series of letters to her confessors that came to light only after her death, Teresa struggled to find words for the spiritual desolation weighing on her. She remarks, for example, that the Cross had become very real to her, as if she herself dangled in agony from it. She frequently refers to the emptiness or darkness within her soul: "Darkness is such that I really do not see—neither with my mind nor with my reason.—The place of God in my soul is blank.—There is no God in me."[5]

When Teresa said, as she frequently did, that there was no God within her, what she most often meant was that she no longer felt God's love. It wasn't that she believed herself hated by God. In some slight way, that might've been comforting, because at least then God would have taken notice of her. No, the knife that twisted in her was her sense that God had for some inexplicable reason grown completely indifferent to her. "God does not want me," she lamented. What made matters worse was her own inability to love God as she had in her youth and middle years. She recognized the folly of pining over the indifference of a God whom she was unable to love herself, but the realization of this "great contradiction" in her life did nothing to alleviate its terrible pain. "I long for God—I want to love Him—to love Him much—to live only for Love of Him—to love only—and yet there is but pain—longing and no love." "The more I want Him—the less I am wanted.—I want to love Him as He has not been loved—and yet there is that separation—that terrible emptiness, that feeling of absence of God." Tuberculosis and cancer, Teresa once plaintively wrote, aren't the "great diseases." A much greater one is to be "unwanted, unloved"—as was, she could've added, the loss of the capacity to love. As the French author Georges Bernanos once noted, hell is the inability to love. Teresa agreed. "If there is a hell," she wrote, "this must be one . . . no prayer—no faith—no love."[6]

How can we understand the darkness which Teresa battled for nearly five full decades? In the Christian spiritual tradition, such crises are not unknown, and they're generally reckoned to fall into two categories. One is called spiritual dryness or acedia, and the other the dark night of the soul. Although many have assumed that Teresa's situation can be understood in terms of one or the other, she herself came to see it as something altogether different.

Spiritual dryness occurs when we find ourselves simply so sick and tired of talking and thinking about God that we're unable to muster the energy or will to pray or worship. It's a state of profound spiritual apathy in which our natural yearning for God dries up and withers. In the first centuries of Christianity, the desert fathers and mothers called this condition the "noontide devil" because it leaves its victims as numbingly exhausted as if baked under a scorching noon sun. The dryness is usually temporary, often gotten through by engaging in some sort of repetitive manual labor. It's unpleasant, because even in the depths of apathy the person suffering from acedia senses that something valuable in her life has gone missing. But the fathers and mothers tended to see it as a state in which an overworked soul can lie fallow for a while until it regains its strength and is once again ready to love God.

The dark night of the soul is something else entirely. Although the phrase was coined by St. John of the Cross in the sixteenth century, the condition long predated his writing about it. Whereas spiritual dryness is a vaguely unpleasant spiritual apathy, the dark night is an excruciatingly desolate sense of God's absence. The person trapped in the dark night longs for God with all his or her might, but discovers that the familiar prayers, devotions, and ways of thinking about God that once sustained now seem lifelessly unable to summon God. A deep loneliness sets in that crushes the will. It's a horrible experience of utter abandonment and total betrayal.

Whereas acedia is a fallow period for the soul, the dark night is a purgation of it—and purgation is always painful, sometimes agonizingly so. During the dark night, our comfortable but distorted and self-serving ideas about God get stripped from us, leaving us in a state that feels like destitution but is actually a cleansing of the soul that prepares it for an experience of the living God. It is, if you will, a spiritual black hole that sucks in everything we once took God to be. Or, put more positively, the agony of the dark night is analogous to birthing pain: agonizing while it lasts, but a preface to great joy.

Teresa's spiritual crisis, although it shares certain characteristics with both acedia and the dark night, doesn't fit easily into either. In the first fifteen years or so of desolation, she herself believed, largely on the advice of her spiritual directors, that she was undergoing a purgative dark night, or possibly even a divine punishment. But eventually she realized that something more profound was going on. "Years back," she wrote in 1961, "—about 17 years now—I wanted to give God something very beautiful.—I bound myself under pain of Mortal Sin not to refuse Him anything.—Since then I have kept this promise—and when sometimes the darkness is very dark—& I am on the verge of saying 'No to God' the thought of that promise pulls me up."[7]

Teresa was referring, of course, to her vow to hold nothing back from Jesus, to give him everything so that he could empty her soul and dwell in her. In reflecting on this vow over the years, she came to believe that Jesus had taken her at her word, and that the darkness she endured was actually a kind of interior, hidden stigmata in which she participated in the desolation felt by Jesus on the Cross: "My God, my God, why have you deserted me?" Her decades of spiritual loneliness were, she concluded, God's acceptance of her vow. She had longed to be so intimate with Christ that her identity would submerge in his. It's just that fusion with his Passion wasn't what she had had in mind.

Teresa also came to another conclusion about the darkness. When she had taken her vows as a Loreto sister, she had assumed the name of the Little Flower because she longed to be one of God's littlest ones. In removing himself from her, God had accepted her "little" status while at the same time giving her something that would allow her to empathize with the poorest of the poor to whom she was called and to always remain humble, no matter how successful her work was. For who was smaller, and who was poorer, than someone abandoned by God?

When Teresa realized all this, she not only meekly accepted the pain of abandonment, but embraced it with a courage that sustained the pledge she'd made to God so many years earlier. She admitted that she couldn't comprehend how her suffering served God. But she accepted on faith that it somehow redounded to God's glory. "Jesus I accept whatever you give—and I give whatever you take."[8]

Although not pretending to know why God would want her to suffer for his sake, Teresa was less uncertain about her suffering's salvific effect on the world. She gradually understood her spiritual darkness in terms of the doctrine of substitutionary atonement, which maintains that the manner in which we deal with our suffering can contribute to the salvation of the world. If we freely embrace it as a participation in the Passion of Jesus, then we give deep meaning to it and join Christ in his redemptive sacrifice. St. Paul laid the foundation for this doctrine when, referring to his own physical infirmities, he wrote, "In my flesh I complete what is lacking in Christ's afflictions for the sake of his body, that is, the Church" (Col 1:24). In sharing Christ's sufferings, in other words, we also share in his glory (Rom 8:17): the salvation of the world. Teresa accepted this. "I am perfectly happy," she once wrote, "if my darkness is light to some soul." "Happy" was probably pushing it too far. But she was certainly willing to suffer if that's what God demanded of her. "Let Him do with me whatever He wants as he wants for as long as He wants."[9]

And this was the key to Teresa's mature spiritual courage. In the first years of her darkness, she displayed the courage to endure her desolate loneliness. But as the decades passed and Teresa came to better understand what was happening to her, she grew into a new and extraordinary form of courage: the courage to *embrace*, and not simply endure, her pain. Endurance is within the reach of many of us. But few follow Teresa when it comes to embracing desolation. For the courage to embrace required that she longed with all her heart to be rid of the pain while simultaneously accepting it as homage to a God who seemed indifferent to her suffering, and whom, truth to tell, she felt unable to love. Yet for all that, God remained God, and Teresa refused to desert him, even if desolation remained her fate for all eternity. "If I ever become a saint," she wrote, "—I will surely be one of 'darkness.' I will continually be absent from heaven—to light the light of those in darkness on earth."[10]

In her last years, Teresa's spiritual darkness was compounded by failing physical health that took her to the brink of death more than once. Shortly before the end, she was admitted to hospital suffering from both cardiac and respiratory failure. Because the doctors had inserted a bronchial tube to help her breathe, she was unable to speak, and for a time was too weak even to write short notes. But finally, after repeated attempts, this frail woman managed to scrawl a three-word message on a slip of paper: "I want Jesus."

Those attending her thought that Teresa was asking for the Eucharist, and undoubtedly she was. But in hindsight, knowing what we do about the spiritual pain that clouded the greater part of her life, her request reads like a plea to finally, at long last, have the darkness lifted. It never was, at least not in the weeks she had left to live. Teresa continued to embrace it, as she believed God wished, to the very end.

20

EVERYDAY COURAGE FOR EVERYDAY CHRISTIANS

there is no fear in love

The courageous Christians profiled in this book are salutary role models whose lives and witness inspire us to be better than we are. But let's be honest: very few of us will ever have to deal with the extreme situations most of them found themselves in. Most probably, none of us will ever face the prospect of dying or being imprisoned or tortured for our faith. It's even unlikely that we'll incur any public scorn to speak of for professing our beliefs. A handful of rude words, an occasional angry rant by a militant atheist: that's about as high a cost as we'll pay for witnessing our faith.

That's not a bad thing. A relatively unruffled life is a great blessing. But we must be careful that we don't take the blessing for granted by falling into the spiritual complacency that Kierkegaard warned about in chapter 1. It's not only the extreme, larger-than-life situations that call for courage. Crammed as it is with both interior and exterior challenges that demand responses from us, everyday life calls for Grace under pressure as well. That's surely part of what Jesus was getting at when he warned that as long as we're in the world, we can expect trials and tribulations (Mk 5:36).

Take the temptation to sin. Every day most of us wrestle with thoughts and desires that, if acted on, are hurtful to ourselves, to others, and to God, and we have to make choices about whether or not to act on them. Although I'm not crazy about the expression, some refer to this constant interior tussle as "spiritual warfare," a struggle with formidable foes—temptations—which are out to seduce us away from our Godlikeness. All of us routinely fight skirmishes in this war, and it takes courage to do so. *Do I claim credit for something I didn't do? Do I gossip about a coworker? Do I betray my significant other? Do I turn a blind eye to an acquaintance in distress? Do I keep the cash-filled wallet I found on the sidewalk, even though the owner's address and phone number is in it? Do I refuse to pray for people I dislike?* To succumb to these temptations is to allow our fear of not being instantly gratified to bully and overrule our better, God-imaged natures, and that's an act of cowardice. To resist temptation is to align our will with God's and to allow Grace under pressure to flow over us.

Of course, resisting temptation is only part of what's required of a Christian disciple. Just as important are the positive responsibilities that faithfulness to Jesus demands, and carrying them out requires courage as well. Jesus taught by example and word that what we do to the least among us we do to him (Matt 25:34–36). When we see a homeless person on the street, for example, do we toss him a few coins and scurry by quickly with head averted so that we don't have to talk to him? Or do we take him to a restaurant, treat him to a meal, and then bring him to our house or apartment for a bath, clean bed, and warm night's sleep? If we balk at the second alternative, chances are good we do so out of fear. *How do I know he won't cut my throat in the middle of the night or steal my possessions?!* Yet Jesus associated freely and happily with all those down-and-out-folks whom the society of his day despised and distrusted. And what if the homeless person to whom we give a bed *does* betray our trust by stealing from us? Remember Bishop Myriel's response to Jean Valjean's thievery in *Les Miserables*? He forgave him. When we, like the good bishop, conform our will to God's, we receive the Grace under pressure to no longer fear the outsider but instead to embrace him or her as a brother or sister. This is courage indeed.

And what about the weariness, cynicism, and sometimes quiet desperation that the sheer grind of life can generate? Day in and day out, it's the same old rut. You drag out of bed in the morning, get the kids off to school, fight the traffic to arrive at a job you don't much like, come home, pay bills or mow the lawn, feed the kids and make sure they do their homework, maybe cap the night off with a bit of mindless television, fall exhausted into bed, and get up again the next morning to do the same thing all over again. Of course our lives are rarely this lackluster and joyless, but the point is that sometimes they feel that way. If we nonetheless persevere, it might be out of an inertia born of hopelessness. But it may also be that our conformity of our will to Christ's literally empowers us to stay the course and serve as he served. Grace under pressure.

Finally, we know that it's quite likely that even humdrum lives will be punctuated with moments of crisis. It's a rare human being who doesn't have to endure the death of someone he or she dearly loves. And all of us, except the very few who will die suddenly or unexpectedly, must one day face our final, fatal illness. These situations will require spiritual as well as moral and physical courage. Grace under pressure will be needed then as, perhaps, never before.

COURAGE AND LOVE

So courage is a necessity even for those of us whose deeds of valor will remain unsung. (Although, come to think of it, Aaron Copland's "Fanfare for the Common Man" actually *does* memorialize the everyday acts of courage that we quietly perform.) The sixty-four-dollar question is how we get to be courageous. The short answer, as we've seen, is conforming our will to God's by accepting the grace bestowed on us, first by virtue of our creation in the divine likeness, second by the coming of the New Adam, Jesus the Christ. But, more specifically, how do we do this?

The key to conforming our will to God's, to so embracing Christ that we want to do nothing other than what will please him, is love. God is love, we're told (1 John 4:8), and growing into our Godlikeness means to dive ever deeper into that love: "God is love, and whoever remains in love remains in God and God in him or her" (John 4:16). We're also told love casts out fear (1 John 4:18). So we are courageous in proportion to how well we love. We receive Grace under pressure to the extent that we love as God loves.

Consider the qualities of love outlined by St. Paul in his First Letter to Corinth (13: 4–7). Love, he says, is patient and kind, never jealous, boastful, conceited, rude, self-serving, easily offended, or resentful. It takes no pleasure in wrongdoing, but finds joy in the good and the true. Finally, says Paul, love is always ready to forgive, to trust, to hope, and to persevere. Every single one of the Christians profiled here fits this description. The depth of their love gave them the courage they needed.

Think about it. Why are we impatient or rude? Generally because we feel threatened by a loss of time, and rudeness is often a defense we use when we're frightened. Jealousy is the fear of not getting something we want or losing something we have. Boastfulness, conceit, and resentment often masquerade quivering insecurity, and the more fragile we feel, the more frantically we focus on our own needs and wants, often to the extent of committing wrongs if we believe that doing so can serve our interests. Underlying all the times in which we fail to love is fear. The implication is that the person who falls victim to a failure to love is a person who hasn't been able to muster the courage to withstand fear. He or she needs, and lacks, Grace under pressure.

But love is so overwhelmingly joyful that it pushes fear to one side. Love, because it's the will of God, gives us the courage to see the world through the eyes of God. We don't trivialize or deny the evil, the suffering, and the pain we encounter in it, but we look upon it all with compassion, able to forgive the harm that others, acting out of their chronic fear, might inflict, trusting that the same divine image that shines forth in us is in them as well, praying that they will discover it, and persevering in our efforts to help them do so. This is the everyday courage with which Grace under pressure gifts us, and it is love that makes us receptive to it.

HABITUATION TO LOVE

So the question of how to become courageous, how to conform one's will to God's, really boils down to the question of how to go about loving.

As creatures made in the image of an all-loving God, you'd think that love would come easily to us. And so it does when we're children. But as we grow and acclimate ourselves to a sometimes harsh world, we frequently forget the love with which and for which we were made and embrace instead any number of substitutes. We begin to think of love as nothing more than a feel-good emotion, thereby reducing it to an utterly subjective, private sensation. This kind of thinking is summed up in the often heard, "Love is just whatever each person thinks it is." Such confusion encourages misconceptions about the nature of love that run from the cynical claim that love is a weakness best avoided, a trap that only suckers fall into, to the thoughtlessly indiscriminate application of the word to anything that pleases: "I love: you, movies, puppies, soft tissues, ice cream, rain," and so on.

But these mutations of love are a far cry from what Paul meant. It's true that love is often associated with a pleasant emotion; but this doesn't mean that it's *identical* to the emotion. Sometimes, as many of us know and as all of the Christians profiled in this book surely did, love actually can be quite painful. Rather than simply being an emotion, love is that state of being which looks with benevolence on the world and wills what is best for it. This, of course, is God's will, and once we conform ourselves to it, the love we begin to experience emboldens us to endure with courage the misfortunes that befall us, to stand up for victims of hatred, and to cling with devoted trust to the source of love, even when we feel desolate and deserted.

The way to go about growing into the love that is our birthright, our privilege, and a necessary condition for Christian courage, is prayerful habituation. To conform to the love that is God, we act lovingly until we begin to genuinely love. Let me explain.

Nearly two and a half millennia ago, the philosopher Aristotle argued that becoming an ethical person required steady perseverance in the calisthenics of virtuous behavior. Go through the motions of practicing the different virtues—patience, prudence, justice, courage, and so on—with day-after-day diligence. It may be hard at first, Aristotle cautioned, and there undoubtedly will be moments of backsliding. But if continued, what originally was an unpleasant task will become pleasurable and second nature: pleasurable because virtuous conduct is more conducive to our long-term well-being than wickedness (a truth some of us learn only through bitter experience), and second nature because after a while virtuous behavior comes easily, almost automatically. The secret to *being* good, then, is habituating oneself to *acting* good.

The same general principle can be applied to reclaiming our ability to love. As a matter of fact, habituating ourselves to love ought to be easier than Aristotle thought habituation to virtue is. He argued that we're not born with virtues, and consequently when we cultivate them we start from scratch. But as we've seen, we're born in the likeness of a supremely lovable and loving God, so habituating ourselves to love is really just clearing away the accumulated rubbish to reach down to the deep core—Christ—within us.

How to go about habituating to love can be learned from Jesus. The first important step is letting go and letting be; the second, to push compassion as far as it will stretch, just as Christ does.

Letting Go and Letting Be

One of the hardest things to do in habituating to love is breaking an old and bad habit that gets in the way of love: viewing ourselves as the center of existence. To a greater or lesser extent, each of us lives in a me-centric universe. Part of the explanation for this is that we're blessed with subjectivity and self-consciousness. We see the world through our own eyes, and we're aware of doing so. Moreover, we continuously carry around our own subjective cosmos of memories, dreams, hopes, fears, fantasies, and so on, for all of which we're the center of gravity. So it only stands to reason that we tend toward egoism. Most of us are idolaters to one extent or another of the great god Me.[1]

One of the problems with this is that it often encourages an invidious judgmentalism in which we either condemn others who don't fall into line the way they're supposed to—which usually means that they behave or look or think differently than we think they ought to—or try to "improve" them by coaxing or badgering them to get in line with the me-universe of which we're the center. Because most of us take ourselves as the gold standard, it rarely occurs to us that others may be judging us even as we judge them, and when we find out, we furiously judge and condemn them for judging us. It would be the stuff of slapstick if it weren't so destructive.

Learning to love means making an effort to see that the diversity we encounter in the world is created by the God who is love, and it is therefore properly cherished rather than condemned. As the Jesuit poet Gerard Manley Hopkins exuberantly cried, "Glory be to God for dappled things," for "All things counter, original, spare, strange," because each and every one of them reveals God: "He fathers-forth [in them] whose beauty is past change."[2] We should let go of our tendency only to approve of things that fit into our own framework, and let be differences—all things counter, original, spare, strange—rather than condemning and rejecting them. This doesn't mean, of course, that we adopt a laissez-faire attitude of cynical indifference to evil, but only that we realize that not everything which is novel or unusual or alien to our way of seeing the world *is* evil. Most of it is very good indeed.

Even Jesus had to learn how to let go and let be. It's one of the most remarkable moments recorded in the Christian scriptures. Jesus is rebuked by a Syrophoenecian woman when he refuses to cast a demon out of her child on the grounds that she's a member of an "unclean" people. It's not good to throw bread intended for children to dogs, he rather callously tells her. Her response? Even dogs deserve crumbs that fall on the floor from the master's table (Mk 7:24–26). Jesus is shamed by her rebuke, and it's at that moment that his ministry of salvation becomes universal. He lets go of his tribal allegiance that promotes the Hebrews at the expense of all other peoples, and lets the Syrophoenecian woman be who she is: a beloved child of God. Henceforth, no more judgmentalism, no more Hebrew-centric field of vision, no more exclusion. The table is open to everyone.

Prayer is one of the best ways to break free of the me-centric universe's gravity field. Praying for persons who are different and with whom one disagrees and maybe even dislikes, asking God's blessing upon them, honestly thanking God for their gifts, and simply resting with them in God's presence, slowly but wonderfully begins to open our hearts to them. The more we pray for someone, the less we can think of them as alien and suspicious, and the more willing—even eager—we are not only to let them be the persons God made them, but to celebrate their uniqueness. And the more we allow them into our me-universe, the more frangible its borders grow, providing Grace the opportunity to flow in.

Pushing Beyond Our Comfort Zone

Habituating ourselves to see with the eyes of God rather than our own me-centric ones doesn't result in an abstract love of everyone. Love is never abstract. It's always targeted, directed toward a specific love object. A cozy Kumbaya attitude that claims to love everyone but never actually touches base with anyone is more sentimentality than love. (Sentimentality is a substitute for love, by the way, that's especially noticeable in our culture. We sob uncontrollably at a Hollywood tear-jerker, but are unmoved by the millions of *real* people living in *real* distress—poverty, homelessness, oppression, and so on—throughout the world.) Letting be looks for the worth in and wishes the best for the members, in all their sometimes messy particularity, of God's wonderfully diverse creation: persons, animals, the earth herself. This is bound to push us beyond the edge of where we feel comfortable. But if the letting go and letting be are genuine, we have to allow them to carry us to places that we might not especially wish to visit, at least not initially.

Jesus, of course, is the obvious go-to example of someone who pushed the envelope in this way. His embrace of the socially marginalized, the pariahs, the unclean, the scoundrels and scallywags and losers of his day, is so well known and so often repeated that it's easy for us to lose sight of just how transformative an act it was. It's comfortable to love our family and our friends but much more difficult and sometimes downright painful to love those who wish us ill or those who come across as . . . well, unlovable. Yet if we wish to conform ourselves to God's will and imitate as closely as humans can his love for us, we're called to love profligately rather than comfortably. No one is beyond the pale of God's love, and this divine inclusiveness is what we should strive for too.

A 2013 photograph of Pope Francis embracing a man with carbuncles and boils that went viral immediately after it appeared on the Internet is a striking visual parable of habituating oneself to a love so profligate that it pushes beyond comfort zones. The pope tenderly holds the man's disfigured face against his own. Many of us gaze at the photograph and squirm with discomfort if not disgust. Francis sees the carbuncles, just like the rest of us do. But he's overcome the human impulse to equate "lovable" with "handsome." He's crossed the border from selective and comfortable compassion to genuine compassion, and in doing so he imitates his Lord, who befriended precisely those people who were "ugly" or "repulsive," physically as well as morally.

Prayer helps us to let go and let be. Rolling up our sleeves and ministering to those who most need it but whom we may find least sympathetic is the trick to stretching our compassion beyond its usual limits. If we can't experience genuine compassion for the horribly disfigured among us at the beginning, imitate it in actual deeds until it becomes the real thing. Leave the secure confines of the "handsome" and go out into the world to seek the "ugly." Be with them, talk with them, touch their wounds, serve them. Of course it will be hard initially. You may make two or three false starts, each time giving the job up as simply too hard. But perseverance softens the heart and expands compassion, and then we receive the gift of loving as God loves. Those people with whom we wouldn't have dreamt of associating, much less loving, become refocused in our field of vision, and we see them as our brothers and sisters, beloved in the eyes of our common divine Parent, beautiful rather than ugly. And then what do we do? We push out again, ever widening the circle of our comfort zone and our love. When we love like this, how could we not be bold? How could we not trust that wherever we go and whomever we encounter, we are in God? And once we experience this Grace under pressure, we have what we need to get through each day.

✿ ✿ ✿

The development of love, and the Grace under pressure that it makes us ever more capable of receiving, is progressive. We will stumble and occasionally fall, but perseverance brings small victories that build on one another. Their cumulative effect slowly cracks the chrysalis of fear that encases us until we emerge as the wondrous creatures made in God's likeness we are.

The anxieties of everyday life will continue to threaten us, and sometimes we may even feel overwhelmed by them. *How am I going to pay the bills? Why doesn't my spouse seem to love me anymore? How do I cope with the medical diagnosis I just received?* But learning to love as God does, learning to conform our will to His by putting off our old self and putting on the Christ-self, empowers us with the confidence that God is with us, come what may. As St. Cyprian said, "Christ gives strength to believers in proportion to the trust that each who receives that strength is willing to place in him."[3] Courage, Grace under pressure, isn't a magic wand that makes bad situations go away. But it does allow us to cope with them by keeping our eye lovingly fixed on God.

Therefore, "Be not afraid!"

NOTES

I. WHO WOULD TRUE VALOR SEE

1. Soren Kierkegaard, *Works of Love*, trans. Howard V. and Edna H. Hong (Princeton, NJ: Princeton University Press, 1998), 479.

2. Ibid., 127.

3. Hemingway seems to have used the expression "grace under pressure" for the first time in a 1926 letter to F. Scott Fitzgerald, reprinted in Carlos Baker (ed.), *Hemingway: Selected Letters, 1917–1961* (New York: Scribner, 1981), 200. Thanks to Tim Allen and Ann Keeler Evans for helping me track down the source. John F. Kennedy quoted Hemingway on the first page of his 1955 *Profiles in Courage*.

4. Ignatius of Antioch, "To the Romans," in *The Epistles of St. Clement of Rome and St. Ignatius of Antioch* (Ancient Christian Writers), trans. James A. Kleist (Mahwah, NJ: Paulist Press, 1978), 82.

5. Quoted in José H. Gomez, *Men of Brave Heart: The Virtue of Courage in the Priestly Life* (Huntingdon, IN: Our Sunday Visitor, 2009), 24.

6. Ernest Hemingway, "A Clean, Well-Lighted Place," in *The Complete Short Stories of Ernest Hemingway* (New York: Scribner, 1998), 291.

2. MICHAEL LAPSLEY

1. Michael Worsnip, *Priest and Partisan: A South African Journey* (Melbourne, Australia: Ocean Press, 1996), 14–15.

2. Ibid., 39.

3. Michael Lapsley, "Dietrich Bonhoeffer and the Struggle for Liberation in Southern Africa," Fifth International Bonhoeffer Conference, Amsterdam (June 1988): 1.

4. Lapsley, "Christians and the Armed Struggle," *Sechaba* (July 1980): 3.

5. Lapsley, *Redeeming the Past: My Journey from Freedom Fighter to Healer* (Maryknoll, NY: Orbis Books, 2012), 75.

6. Ibid., 120.

7. Worsnip, *Priest and Partisan,* 146.

8. Ibid., 31.

9. Lapsley, BBC interview (13 April 1995).

10. Lapsley, *Redeeming the Past*, 244.

11. Ibid., 11.

12. Worsnip, *Priest and Partisan*, 143.

3. THE FRATERNAL MARTYRS OF BURUNDI

1. Frederick Quinn, *African Saints: Saints, Martyrs, and Holy People from the Continent of Africa* (New York: Crossroad, 2002), 136.

2. "Buta: Brothers for Life or Death," documentary (2013). http://www.youtube.com/watch?v=ZeArNZ85iB4. See also "Umuvukano (Fraternity)," documentary (2012). http://www.youtube.com/watch?v=7Qftw2ZCeXs.

3. Ibid.

4. John L. Allen, Jr., *The Global War on Christians: Dispatches from the Front Line of Anti-Christian Persecution* (New York: Image, 2013), 223.

5. "Buta: Brothers for Life or Death."

6. Quinn, *African Saints*, 137.

7. For a refutation of this position, see Allen, *Global War*, 223–26.

8. Ibid., 225.

4. DOROTHY STANG

1. Michele Murdock, *A Journey of Courage: The Amazing Story of Sister Dorothy Stang* (Cincinnati, OH: Sisters of Notre Dame de Namur, 2009), 108.

2. Murdock, *Journey of Courage*, 107; Roseanne Murphy, *Martyr of the Amazon: The Life of Sister Dorothy Stang* (Maryknoll, NY: Orbis, 2007), 122.

3. Murdock, *Journey of Courage*, 62.

4. Murphy, *Martyr of the Amazon*, 57.

5. Ibid., 84.

6. Murdock, *Journey of Courage*, 83.

7. Murphy, *Martyr of the Amazon*, 131.

8. Ibid., 123.

9. Murdock, *Journey of Courage*, 87.

10. Ibid., 90.

11. The trials of Stang's assassins are discussed in the documentary "They Killed Sister Dorothy." Just Media, 2008, DVD.

12. Murdock, *Journey of Courage*, 101.

13. Binka Le Breton, *The Greatest Gift: The Courageous Life and Martyrdom of Sister Dorothy Stang* (New York: Doubleday, 2007), 225.

5. ALEXANDER MEN

1. Quoted in David Conway, "What Is to Be Done with Lenin's Remains?" (February 4, 2013), http://www.libertylawsite.org/2013/02/04/what-is-to-be-done-with-lenins-remains. Lenin wrote his denunciation in a 1913 letter to Maxim Gorky.

2. Yves Hamant, *Alexander Men: A Witness for Contemporary Russia*, trans. Fr. Steven Bigham (Torrance, CA: Oakwood, 1995), 49.

3. Ibid., 145.

4. Alexander Men, "The Russian Orthodox Church Today," in Elizabeth Roberts and Ann Shukman (eds.), *Christianity for the Twenty-First Century: The Prophetic Writings of Alexander Men* (New York: Continuum, 1996), 167.

5. Alexander Men, "Christianity for the Twenty-First Century," in Roberts and Shukman, 185.

6. Ibid., 189.

7. Alexander Men, "Religion and the Secular State," in Roberts and Shukman, 121, 122.

8. Alexander Men, "Russia in Crisis," in Roberts and Shukman, 143.

9. Hamant, *Alexander Men*, 204.

10. Ibid., 141.

11. Ibid., 5.

12. Ibid., 138.

13. Ibid.

14. Men, "Christianity for the Twenty-First Century," 182.

15. Alexander Men, *Awake to Life! Sermons from the Paschal Cycle*, trans. Maria Sapiets (Torrance, CA: Oakwood, 1996), 62.

6. THE TIBHIRINE MONKS

1. John W. Kiser, *The Monks of Tibhirine: Faith, Love, and Terror in Algeria* (New York: St. Martin's Griffin, 2002), 156.

2. Ibid., 232.

3. Ibid., 67–68.

4. Ibid., 174.

5. Ibid., 197.

6. Bernardo Olivera, OCSO, *How Far to Follow? The Martyrs of Atlas* (Kalamazoo, MI: Cistercian Publications, 1997), 55.

7. Olivera, *How Far?*, 55–76; Kiser, *Monks of Tibhirine*, 145–49.

8. Kiser, *Monks of Tibhirine*, 203.

9. Olivera, *How Far?*, 58, 157, 103.

10. Ibid., 103.

11. Olivera, *How Far?*, 98. Kiser, *Monks of Tibhirine*, 220, 169.

12. Kiser, *Monks of Tibhirine*, 213.

13. Olivera, *How Far?*, 127.

14. Ibid., 127, 129.

15. Ibid., 36.

16. Ibid., 35.

7. MYCHAL JUDGE

1. Salvatore Sapienza, *Mychal's Prayer* (n.p.: Tregatti Press, 2011), 86.

2. Michael Ford, *Father Mychal Judge: An Authentic American Hero* (New York: Paulist Press, 2002), 27.

3. Congregation for the Propagation of the Faith, *Letter to the Bishops of the Catholic Church on the Pastoral Care of Homosexuals* (October 1, 1986), paragraph 3.

4. Ford, *Father Mychal Judge*, 124.

5. "The Saint of 9/11: The True Story of Father Mychal Judge." Arts Alliance American Films, 2006, DVD.

6. Michael Daly, *The Book of Mychal* (New York: St. Martin's Press, 2008), 257.

7. Sapienza, *Mychal's Prayer*, 28.

8. "The Saint of 9/11."

9. Ford, *Father Mychal Judge*, 12.

10. Ibid., 13.

11. Ibid., 82.

8. RUTH MANORAMA

1. Elze Sietzema-Riemer, *Christian Dalits* (Universiteit Utrecht: Taal-en Cultuurstudies, 2009), http://www.indianet.nl/pdf/christiandalits.pdf.

2. Sudha Umashanker, "A Relentless Crusader," *The Hindu,* July 23, 2011.

3. Nirmala Carvalho, "Christian Woman from Tamil Nadu Receives Award for Her Fight on Behalf of Dalit Women," *AsiaNews*, September 29, 2006.

4. Quoted by Manorama in her acceptance speech, 2006 Right Livelihood Award, http://www.rightlivelihood.org/manorama_speech.html.

5. Umashanker, "A Relentless Crusader."

6. Teesta Setalvad, "Power within the Church Still Lies with the Upper Castes," interview with Ruth Manorama, *Communalism Combat*, December 2000, http://www.sabrang.com/cc/comold/dec00/cover5.htm.

7. Ibid.

8. Ibid.

9. Manorama, Acceptance Speech, 2006 Right Livelihood Award.

9. SHAHBAZ BHATTI

1. Mahendra Prasad Singh and Himanshu Roy (eds.), *Indian Political Thought: Themes and Thinkers* (Delhi: Pearson, 2011), 148.

2. Rupert Shortt, *Christianophobia: A Faith Under Attack* (London: Rider Books, 2012), 64.

3. Jibran Khan, "Punjab: Acquittal for 70 Muslim Defendants on Trial for the Gojra Massacre," *AsiaNews.it* (November 6, 2011), http://www.asianews.it/news-en/Punjab:-acquittal-for-70-Muslim-extremists-on-trial-for-the-Gojra-massacre-21805.html.

4. Michelle A. Vu, "Q&A: Pakistan's Minister for Minorities Shahbaz Bhatti," *Christian Post* (February 8, 2011), http://www.christianpost.com/news/qa-pakistans-minister-for-minorities-shahbaz-bhatti-48894.

5. Anonymous, "Shahbaz Bhatti, a Catholic, Is the New Minister for the Defense of Minorities," *AsiaNews.it* (April 11, 2008), http://www.asianews.it/news-en/Shahbaz-Bhatti,-a-Catholic,-is-the-new-minister-for-the-defense-of-minorities-13664.html.

6. John L. Allen, Jr., "Recognize Martyrs around the World by Canonizing One of Their Own," *National Catholic Reporter* (May 4, 2012), http://ncronline.org/blogs/all-things-catholic/recognize-martyrs-around-world-canonizing-one-their-own.

7. Vu, "Q&A: Pakistan's Minister for Minorities Shahbaz Bhatti."

8. Anonymous, "Pakistan Minorities Minister Shahbaz Bhatti Shot Dead,"
BBC News South Asia (March 2, 2011), http://www.bbc.co.uk/news/world-south-asia-12617562.

9. Ibid.

10. Shortt, *Christianophobia*, 82.

11. Annabelle Bentham, "Shahbaz Bhatti Obituary," *The Guardian* (March 10, 2011), http://www.guardian.co.uk/world/2011/mar/10/shahbaz-bhatti-obituary.

10. THE NICKEL MINES AMISH

1. Donald B. Kraybill, Steven M. Nolt, and David L. Weaver-Zercher, *Amish Grace: How Forgiveness Transcended Tragedy* (San Francisco, CA: Jossey-Bass, 2007), 25.

2. Ibid.

3. Ibid., 49.

4. Ibid., 132.

5. The critics included David Gottlieb, "Not Always Divine," *Cross-Currents* (October 17, 2006), http://www.cross-currents.com/archives/2006/10/17/not-always-divine; Jeff Jacoby, "Undeserved Forgiveness," *The Boston Globe* (October 8, 2006); and John Podhoretz, "Hating a Child Killer," *National Review* (October 5, 2006), http://www.nationalreview.com/corner/129694/hating-child-killer/john-podhoretz.

6. Kraybill et al., *Amish Grace*, 115.

7. Ibid., 120.

8. Donald B. Kraybill, Steven M. Nolt, and David L. Weaver-Zercher, *The Amish Way: Patient Faith in a Perilous World* (San Francisco, CA: Jossey-Bass, 2010), 160.

9. Thieleman J. van Braght, *Martyrs Mirror*, trans. Joseph F. Sohm (Scottsdale, OH: Herald Press, 2004), 741. Originally published in 1660.

11. LI YING

1. China Aid, "2012 Annual Report: Chinese Government Persecution of Christians and Churches in Mainland China," https://docs.google.com/file/d/0B_YUgSyiG6aIWUpXdWwtWVJWb00/edit?pli=1.

2. "Document of the General Office of the Central Committee of the Communist Party of China 18 (2011)," https://docs.google.com/file/d/0B_ YUgSyiG6aIOU9VMndERXUwN00/edit?pli=1.

3. U.S. Department of State, "International Religious Freedom Report for 2012," http://www.state.gov/j/drl/rls/irf/religiousfreedom/index.htm#wrapper.

4. China Aid/Monitor China, "Testimony of Sister Li Ying," September 10, 2003, http://monitorchina.org/en_show.php?id=117.

5. Li Ying's mug shot can be found on her "Prisoner Profile," at Voice of the Martyrs: PrisonerAlert website, http://www.prisoneralert.com/pprofiles/ vp_prisoner_111_profile.html.

12. EMIL KAPAUN

1. Roy Wenzl and Travis Heying, *The Miracle of Father Kapaun: Priest, Soldier, and Korean War Hero* (San Francisco: Ignatius Press, 2013), 92.

2. Katherine Miller, "Army Chaplain Emil Kapaun Received Medal of Honor," *The Washington Free Beacon* (April 11, 2013), http://freebeacon.com/ army-chaplain-emil-kapaun-to-receive-medal-of-honor.

3. Wenzl and Heying, *Miracle of Father Kapaun*, 76.

4. Ibid., 54.

5. William L. Maher, *A Shepherd in Combat Boots: Chaplain Emil Kapaun of the 1st Cavalry Division* (Shippensburg, PA: Burd Street Press, 1997), 145.

6. Ibid., 60.

7. John Pronechen, "For God and Country," *National Catholic Register* (April 16, 2013), http://www.ncregister.com/site/article/for-god-and-country/ #ixzz2XX8ALKur.

8. "The Miracle of Father Kapaun." Ignatius Press, 2010, DVD.

13. CLARENCE JORDAN

1. "Briars in the Cotton Patch: The Story of Koinonia Farm." Cotton Patch Productions, 2003, DVD.

2. Joyce Hollyday (ed.), *Clarence Jordan: Essential Writings* (Maryknoll, NY: Orbis Books, 2003), 21.

3. Henlee H. Barnette, *Clarence Jordan: Turning Dreams into Deeds* (Macon, GA: Smith & Helwys, 1992).

4. Hollyday, *Clarence Jordan*, 17.

5. Ibid., 16.

6. Barnette, *Clarence Jordan: Turning Dreams into Deeds*, 6.

7. Hollyday, *Clarence Jordan*, 120.

8. Ibid., 118.

14. DIANNA ORTIZ

1. *Guatemala Memory of Silence: Report of the Commission of Historical Clarification: Conclusions and Recommendations* (Guatemala City: Litoprint, 1999), 20.

2. Dianna Ortiz with Patricia Davis, *The Blindfold's Eyes: My Journey from Torture to Truth* (Maryknoll, NY: Orbis, 2002), 20.

3. Julia Lieblich, "Pieces of Bone," *Agni Online* 47 (1998), http://www.webdelsol.com/AGNI/asp98jl2.htm.

4. Dianna Ortiz, "US Nun Tortured in Central America Recalls the Nightmare," *Truthout* (March 12, 2012), http://truth-out.org/index.php?option=com_k2&view=item&id=7227:us-nun-tortured-in-central-america-recalls-the-nightmare.

5. Ortiz, *Blindfold's Eyes*, 65.

6. Ibid., 73.

7. Ibid., 80.

8. Ibid.

9. Ibid., 71.

10. Ibid., 53.

11. Ibid., 132.

12. Ibid.

13. Ibid., 474.

14. Ibid., 475.

15. WALTER CISZEK

1. Walter J. Ciszek with Daniel L. Flaherty, *With God in Russia* (New York: Image, 1966), 18.

2. Ibid., 105.

3. Walter J. Ciszek with Daniel L. Flaherty, *He Leadeth Me* (San Francisco: Ignatius Press, 1995), 42, 51.

4. Ibid., 68.

5. Ibid., 75.

6. Ibid., 75–76.

7. Ibid., 76.

8. Ibid., 39.

9. Ibid.

10. Ibid., 158.

16. THEA BOWMAN

1. Charlene Smith and John Feister, *Thea's Song: The Life of Thea Bowman* (Maryknoll, NY: Orbis Books, 2009), 249.

2. Maurice J. Nutt (ed.), *Thea Bowman: In My Own Words* (Liguori, MI: Liguori Publications, 2009), 4.

3. Smith and Feister, *Thea's Song*, 26.

4. Thea Bowman, *Shooting Star: Selected Writings and Speeches*, ed. Celestine Cepress (Winona, MN: Saint Mary's Press/Christian Brothers Publications, 1993), 21.

5. Smith and Feister, *Thea's Song*, 55; Bowman, *Shooting Star*, 94, 23.

6. Bowman, *Shooting Star*, 65.

7. Ibid., 45.

8. *The Voice of Negro America* (Canton, MI: Holy Child Jesus School, 1967), LP record.

9. Bowman, *Shooting Star*, 32.

10. Smith and Feister, *Thea's Song*, 96, 237.

11. Bowman, *Shooting Star*, 107.

12. Smith and Feister, *Thea's Song*, 224.

13. Bowman, *Shooting Star*, 19.

17. C. S. LEWIS

1. Walter Hooper, *C. S. Lewis: A Complete Guide to His Life and Works* (San Francisco: HarperSanFrancisco, 1996), 65.

2. C. S. Lewis, *A Grief Observed* (New York: HarperOne, 2000), 30.

3. Ibid., 11, 15.

4. Ibid., 20.

5. Ibid., 6.

6. Ibid., 64.

7. Ibid., 54.

8. Ibid., 46.

9. Ibid., 64.

10. Ibid., 69.

11. Lewis to Mrs. Arnold, November 21, 1962, in Walter Hooper (ed.), *Letters of C. S. Lewis*, rev. ed. (New York: Harcourt Brace, 1993), 506.

18. HENRI NOUWEN

1. Henri J. M. Nouwen, *The Inner Voice of Love: A Journey through Anguish to Freedom* (New York: Doubleday, 1996), 3.

2. Michael Ford, *Wounded Prophet: A Portrait of Henri J. M. Nouwen* (New York: Doubleday, 1999), 92.

3. Nouwen, *Inner Voice*, xiii.

4. Ibid., xvii.

5. Henri J. M. Nouwen, *The Wounded Healer* (New York: Doubleday, 1972), 84.

6. Nouwen, *Inner Voice*, 26.

7. Ibid., 88.

19. MOTHER TERESA

1. Mother Teresa, *Come Be My Light: The Private Writings of the "Saint of Calcutta,"* ed. Brian Kolodiejchuk (New York: Doubleday, 2007), 210.

2. Ibid., 29.

3. Renzo Allegri, *Teresa of the Poor* (Ann Arbor, MI: Servant Publications, 1998), 53.

4. Mother Teresa, *Be My Light*, 187.

5. Ibid., 210.

6. Ibid., 210, 164, 296, 250.

7. Ibid., 210–11.

8. Ibid., 225.

9. Ibid., 212.

10. Ibid., 230.

20. EVERYDAY COURAGE FOR
EVERYDAY CHRISTIANS

1. I explore this and other forms of idolatry in *Giving Up god . . . to Find God: Breaking Free of Idolatry* (Maryknoll, NY: Orbis Books, 2013).

2. Gerard Manley Hopkins, "Pied Beauty," in *Poems and Prose*, ed. W. H. Gardner (New York: Penguin, 1984), 30, 31.

3. Quoted in José H. Gomez, *Men of Brave Heart: The Virtue of Courage in the Priestly Life* (Huntingdon, IN: Our Sunday Visitor, 2009), 189.

INDEX

African National Congress, 15, 18–19
"Alejandro". *See* Ortiz, Dianna, kidnapping and torture
Alinksy, Saul, 68
apartheid, 16, 17
Armed Islamic Group, 47, 48, 51–53. *See also* Tibhirine monks
atheism in Soviet Union, 39, 39–40

Bakuru, Father Zacharie, 25, 26, 27, 28
Ball, Nathan, 155, 157
Bhatti, Shahbaz, 73–80; and All Pakistan Minority Alliance, 76; and Pakistan blasphemy laws, 73–77; assassination of, 78–79; as cabinet minister for minorities, 76–78; case for canonization, 79–80
Bhutto, Zulfikar Ali, 74
Bibi, Aasia, 75. *See also* Batti, Shahbaz, and Pakistan blasphemy laws
Boisen, Anton, 152
Bowman, Thea, 135–141; and black spirituality, 136, 137–138; and Franciscan Sisters of Perpetual Adoration, 136–137; and interracial reconciliation, 139, 141; as teacher, 137–139; illness and death, 135, 139–141; on love, 135, 139, 141
Bunyan, John, 1, 2
Burundi: aftermath of massacre, 28–29; genocide in, 24, 25; Le Petit Seminaire

de St-Paul, 24; martyrs of, 23–29; massacre of students, 26–27
Bush, George H. W., 119, 123

Catholic Theological Institute (Utrecht), 153
Ciszek, Walter, 127–134; as "tough guy," 127–128; in gulag, 133; in Lubyanka Prison, 129–133; spiritual crisis, 130–132; underground ministry in Soviet Union, 128, 129, 133–134
Clinton, Bill, 123
Copland, Aaron, 169
courage: and faith, 2; and fear, 167–169, 175; and letting go, letting be, 172–173; and love, 169–172; and prayer, 173; as Grace under pressure, 4, 4–8, 169, 175; as guts, 3–4, 5; Jesus as prototype, 8; types of, 7–8, 10–11

Dalits, 65–66. *See also* Manorama, Ruth
Davidman, Joy. *See* Lewis, C. S.
Day, Dorothy, 110
de Cherche, Christian. *See* Tibhirine monks, profiles of
Dochier, Luc. *See* Tibhirine monks, profiles of

Eisenhower, Dwight D., 110
England, Martin, 107, 108

Favre-Miville, Paul. *See* Tibhirine monks, profiles of

Fleury, Michel. *See* Tibhirine monks, profiles of

fraternal martyrs of Burundi. *See* Burundi, martyrs of

Freire, Paolo, 68

Fuller, Millard, 112. *See also* Jordan, Clarence, and Habitat for Humanity

Giuliani, Rudy, 59, 60

Gojra massacre, 74. *See also* Bhatti, Shahbaz

Gong Shengliang, 92, 95, 95–96

Gregory of Nyssa, 6

Harvard University, 153, 154

Hemingway, Ernest, 3, 4, 5, 8

Huddleston, Trevor, 16

Ignatius of Antioch, 4

Jesus, 8, 23, 27, 67–68, 78, 85, 86, 112, 131, 139, 168, 173, 174

Jordan, Clarence, 105–113; and Habitat for Humanity, 112; and Koinonia Farm, 107–112; death of, 112–113; early ministry of, 106–107; hostility against, 109–112; on fear and courage, 106, 111–112

Judge, Mychal, 55–62; and TWA Flight 800, 59; as FDNY chaplain, 55, 60; death on 9/11, 55, 60–61; gay ministry of, 57–58; generosity of, 58, 59

Kapaun, Emil, 97–104; death of, 104; decorations for valor, 97–98, 99; in POW camp, 101–103; military service in Korea, 99–100; military service in WWII, 99

Kennedy, Robert, 134

Kierkegaard, Soren, 2, 11, 167

Kolbe, Maximilian, 55

Krautler, Edwin, 35, 36, 38

Lapsley, Michael, 15–21; abandons pacifism, 16–18, 19; and Institute for Healing of Memories, 21; and

Theological Exchange Programme, 20, 21; attempted assassination of, 15, 21

Lebreton, Christophe. *See* Tibhirine monks, profiles of

Lee, Harper, 3

Lemarchand, Christian. *See* Tibhirine monks, profiles of

Lenin, Vladimir Ilych, 39

Les Miserables (Victor Hugo), 168

Lewis, C. S., 143–150; and Joy Davidman, 143–145; grief and despair, 145, 146, 147; on absence, 145–146; on God, 146–147; recovery, 147–149

Lewis, Warnie, 144

Li Ying, 89–96; and religious repression in China, 89–91, 96; and South China Church, 91–92; imprisonment of, 95–96; ministry of, 92–95

Malik, Alexander John, 78

Mandela, Nelson, 20

Manorama, Ruth, 65–71; advocate for Dalits, 66–69; and Dalit women, 68, 69; and Indian church, 70–71; leadership of Christian Dalit Liberation Movement, 69; National Federation of Dalit Women, 69; wins Right Livelihood Award, 71; Women's Voice, 69

McGreevy, Robert, 97, 104

Men, Alexander, 39–46; assassination of, 45; as spiritual guide, 41–43, 46; as writer, 41; Jewish background, 40, 44; persecution of, 41, 44; trained in catacomb church, 40

Menninger Clinic, 152

Missionaries of Charity, 159, 161

Mother Teresa, 80, 159–165; and acedia, 163; and dark night of the soul, 163; and Sisters of Loreto, 160, 161; and substitutionary atonement, 164–165; her spiritual dryness, 159, 162–165

National Black Sisters Conference, 138

Naudet, Jules, 61

Ndayisaba, Carter, 26

Nickel Mines Amish, 81–88; Amish notion of forgiveness, 84–87; and Anabaptist roots, 81, 82, 86–87; assault on school,

82–83; media coverage of, 84–85; *Uffgevva* , 86–87, 88
NKVD, 129, 130, 134
Nouwen, Henri, 151–158; his restlessness, 153–154; on First Love, 157–158; on woundedness, 151–152, 155; spiritual crisis, 155–156; Work at L'Arche, 154–155

Olivera, Dom Bernardo, 47, 54
Ortiz, Dianna, 117–124; human rights advocacy, 123–124; kidnapping and torture, 119–120; on courage, 124; spiritual crisis, 122–123, 124

Pope Francis, 174

Reagan, Ronald, 119
Rembrandt van Rijn, 157
Ringeard, Celestin. *See* Tibhirine monks, profiles of
Roberts, Charles Carl IV. *See* Nickel Mines Amish, assault on school
Rusimbamigera, Jolique, 27, 29
Rwanda, genocide, 24

School of the Americas, 117, 124
Sermon on the Mount, 23, 107, 108
Sisters of Notre Dame de Namur, 31
Soosairaj, Bama Faustina, 68
Soweto massacre, 17

Stalin, Joseph, 40
Stang, Dorothy, 31–38; advocates for small farmers, 31–120; assassination of, 32, 38; environmentalism of, 35–37; ministry in Brazil, 33–34
Su Casa Catholic Worker House (Chicago), 122, 123

Taseer, Salmann, 75, 78
Teresa of Calcutta. *See* Mother Teresa
Tibhirine monks, 47–54; and attitude to Islam, 47, 49, 50, 51, 52, 53–54; and Islamicist violence against, 51–54; assassinations of, 47, 53; Our Lady of Atlas monastery, 48, 48–49; profiles of, 48–51; testament of Christian de Cherche, 53–54
Torture Abolition and Survivors Support Coalition International (TASSC), 124

ul-Haq, Zia, 74
Universal Declaration of Human Rights, 74

Vanier, Jean, 154

Williams, Rowan, 74

Xu, Peter, 91

Yale University, 153